Statutory Nuisance and Residential Property

Statutory Nuisance and Residential Property: Environmental Health Problems in Housing examines the statutory nuisance provisions in the Environmental Protection Act 1990 pertaining to the condition of premises and related problems in housing and compares these with the provisions of the Housing Act 2004. The book discusses the separate development of statutory nuisance and housing legislation in an historic context, which provides a useful basis for the understanding and interpretation of legislation and the different remedies available today. The work includes a chapter on actions by "persons aggrieved" using section 82 of the Environmental Protection Act 1990 and also considers remedies provided in the Anti-social Behaviour, Crime and Policing Act 2014.

This book:

- investigates housing problems in the context of the relevant law; and
- demonstrates how to use the legal framework appropriately and be able to decide on the most appropriate provision for dealing with environmental health problems associated with residential property.

This is an essential and practical book for environmental health and housing professionals, as well as for advisers and lawyers in the private and public housing sectors.

Stephen Battersby is a freelance environmental health and housing consultant and fellow of the CIEH and RSPH. He is a past president of the CIEH and currently vice president. He has chaired the Pro Housing Alliance, ARCHIVE UK (Architecture for Health in Vulnerable Environments), and Generation Rent (National Tenants Organisation). Currently he chairs the Committee of Management of the National Code of Standards for larger student developments. His research interests include housing conditions and health (housing as a social determinant of health), the use and enforcement of legislation to secure healthful housing, and urban rodent infestations and public health. He is also the current editor of *Clay's Handbook of Environmental Health* – the standard environmental health textbook.

In 2014 he was awarded an MBE in the Birthday Honours List for services to Environmental Health.

John Pointing is a barrister practising in environmental health law. His practice includes advising and representing local authorities, central government, commercial clients, and private individuals. He is the Legal Partner of Statutory Nuisance Solutions, a firm he set up with David Horrocks in 2010.

Since 1992, he has run courses for the Chartered Institute of Environmental Health and for local authorities on a wide range of issues, including statutory nuisance, food safety and health and safety. From 2003 to 2013, he was a senior lecturer in law at Kingston University. He is a visiting lecturer at several universities and an external examiner at De Montfort University for environmental law and food law.

He is co-author (with Rosalind Malcolm) of the leading text on statutory nuisance law: *Statutory Nuisance Law and Practice* (2nd ed., 2011) and *Food Safety Enforcement* (2005). Since 2003, he has been interested in issues affecting the Muslim community, particularly those to do with fake Halal and food crime.

Routledge Focus on Environmental Health
Series Editor: Stephen Battersby, MBE PhD, FCIEH, FRSPH

Statutory Nuisance and Residential Property

Environmental Health Problems in Housing

Stephen Battersby and John Pointing

Routledge
Taylor & Francis Group
LONDON AND NEW YORK

Chartered Institute of
Environmental Health

First published 2019
by Routledge
4 Park Square, Milton Park, Abingdon, Oxon OX14 4RN
605 Third Avenue, New York, NY 10017

First issued in paperback 2023

Routledge is an imprint of the Taylor & Francis Group, an informa business

British Library Cataloguing-in-Publication Data
A catalogue record for this book is available from the British Library

Library of Congress Cataloging-in-Publication Data
Names: Battersby, Stephen, 1949– author. | Pointing, John, author.
Title: Statutory nuisance and residential property : environmental
   health problems in housing / Stephen Battersby and John
   Pointing.
Description: Abingdon, Oxon ; New York, NY : Routledge, 2019. |
   Series: Routledge focus on environmental health
Identifiers: LCCN 2019003980 | ISBN 9781138338135 (hardback :
   alk. paper) | ISBN 9780429441912 (ebook)
Subjects: LCSH: Housing—Law and legislation—England. |
   Nuisances—England. | Housing and health—England. |
   Housing—Environmental aspects—England.
Classification: LCC KD1179 .B38 2019 | DDC 344.4204/6—dc23
LC record available at https://lccn.loc.gov/2019003980

ISBN: 978-1-03-257050-1 (pbk)
ISBN: 978-1-138-33813-5 (hbk)
ISBN: 978-0-429-44191-2 (ebk)

DOI: 10.1201/9780429441912

Typeset in Times New Roman
by Apex CoVantage, LLC

Publisher's Note
The publisher has gone to great lengths to ensure the quality of this reprint but points out that some imperfections in the original copies may be apparent.

Contents

Preface

For more than twenty-five years, both of us have carried out training for local authority housing and environmental health officers in law and professional practice. This book is the product of this training and also our other roles in advising on public policy, as well as working with local authorities, commercial bodies, and the Chartered Institute of Environmental Health (CIEH).

A complex body of law and regulation has grown up over many years, which local authorities have struggled to implement. Cuts to their budgets and a declining skills base for inspection and regulation have exposed local authorities to the risk of failure in fulfilling their statutory duties. Housing policy is also very political and prone to catastrophic errors. On the front page of *The Observer*, published on 20 January 2019, is a report based on a Freedom of Information request, which states that 40% of council homes sold in London to tenants under "Margaret Thatcher's totemic right-to-buy scheme" are now in the hands of private landlords. This policy is linked to the low levels of provision of social housing and is justly considered by many to have been a disaster.

Since 2010, the decline of state regulation in housing and as a means of protecting public health and safety has become painfully apparent. The tragedy of the Grenfell Tower disaster of June 2017 will probably be judged in the light of multiple regulatory failures once the report of Sir Martin Moore-Bick is completed. The origins of present-day regulatory problems go back to the deregulation initiatives of the 1990s. The Deregulation and Contracting Out Act 1994 was enacted partly in order to simplify legislation that had accumulated over many years and had resulted in complexity and unnecessary burdens being placed on business. The totemic cause of deregulation subsequently became something akin to a religious cult, with civil servants incentivised to add to a metaphorical bonfire of regulations thought by government to be merely burdensome. It is worth recalling the venom with which the deregulation initiative started. Neil Hamilton, the

Deregulation Minister in John Major's Government, addressed the Conservative Party conference in 1994 by describing the role of enforcement officers as: "Handmaidens of business – helping them to comply – rather than the local branch of the Gestapo" (*Weekly Telegraph*, 118, 1994).

We believe that much of the policy surrounding the deregulation agenda and over centralisation of public administration has been misconceived. The determination to roll back the frontiers of the state and to instil the virtues of the private market has been largely rhetorical, benefiting some individuals but exposing many to the deficiencies in the system of provision of adequate and affordable social housing. The aim of this book is to encourage local authorities to use their powers in respect of housing problems better and for government to take a more nuanced lead over regulation, never forgetting that local government's origins lie in safeguarding the public's health and effective use of the law is one of the mechanisms for achieving that.

Stephen Battersby and John Pointing
21 January 2019

Table of cases

Tables of legislation

Table of primary legislation

Table of secondary legislation

1 Introduction

1.01 The work of environmental health and housing practitioners, including advisers, often means that they are facing problems and issues that potentially have several routes by which a remedy can be found. It is a general claim that environmental health officers (EHOs) or environmental health practitioners (EHPs) are public health "problem solvers". Practitioners working for and on behalf of local authorities need to have a legal basis for any actions to resolve these problems; at the same time, there are overlaps and contradictions between different pieces of legislation. This can lead to dilemmas as to what is the most appropriate course of action. It can also lead to confusion and indeed errors when aspects of the different legal provisions become combined or confused and the correct procedure not followed. In many, if not most cases, it is not possible for a practitioner to "read across" from one legal provision to another. This means that the practitioner and environmental health manager needs a clear understanding of the relevant legal provisions both to ensure that the appropriate basis for action is chosen but also to ensure that there is no mixing of different legal procedures (although, as will be shown later, there is nothing to prevent the different provisions being used for different problems in the same premises, where appropriate).

1.02 It has also often been argued that EHOs choose to resolve problems by persuasion and by taking an "informal" approach. Whatever the merits of this – and for residential property there will be a concern that this approach can leave vulnerable tenants exposed to unresolved issues for long periods – should such efforts fail, then recourse to legal remedies will become necessary.

1.03 This monograph is aimed at helping practitioners investigate problems associated with residential property, in particular, conditions in and around dwellings. It also aims to help practitioners use the legal framework appropriately and to be able to choose the most appropriate provision for enforcement. It also provides legal practitioners and housing advisers with an overview of the relevant legal provisions.

1.04   One might ask, why is this work needed – given that since the mid-nineteenth century, EHOs have traditionally used statutory nuisance to deal with a range of problems, including those in and around premises? For a start it is apparent that the housing market has undergone substantial changes in recent years. For example, since 2011, the number of households in the private rented sector (PRS) has increased by about 30%, and the private rented sector is now substantially larger than the social housing sector.[1] This change has occurred to such an extent that it could be argued that parts of the PRS fulfil some of the same functions as the social housing sector. The distinction is becoming blurred, given that local authorities can meet their duties under homelessness legislation by way of a PRS offer, which may not even be in the same borough.

1.05   At the same time, a recent study[2] has found that a surprisingly large minority of local authorities do not employ any qualified EHOs for inspecting dwellings. In many authorities, even where EHOs are employed, other officers carry out much of this work. The qualifications of these non-EHOs, their experience and knowledge are unknown and are likely to vary from council to council. Whether or not these less qualified officers are working under the direction of an EHO who understands the legal provisions available to them, this monograph aims to help them in practical ways. It is also hoped that it will help others who advise on housing problems. Action is required to address poor housing conditions, for it has been estimated that poor housing costs the NHS in England £1.4 billion per year,[3] and this is without including "exported" and social costs due to days off work or out of school. This figure is probably an underestimate as it takes little account of the effects of poor housing on mental health and wellbeing.

1.06   An analysis of statutory nuisance is provided in this work. Although an old concept, it has value in certain situations, though it is apparent that many environmental health practitioners are not using or are unaware of the statutory nuisance provisions provided in Part III of the Environmental Protection Act 1990 (EPA 1990). In particular, s.79(1)(a) of the EPA 1990 is important for dealing with nuisance and health risks associated with premises, particularly domestic premises. An assumption is often made that any issue associated with housing is solely a matter for the Housing Act 2004 (HA 2004). But there is a clear overlap between this legislation and the statutory nuisance provisions of the EPA 1990 and related provisions. As an illustration of a "siloed" approach, there have been times when how a local authority dealt with a complaint depended on which department had received it. A selective policy on which legislation to use has subsisted even where EHOs have been employed in both "housing" and "environmental health" departments. EHOs employed in the former would think solely in terms of Housing Act remedies, whilst only those in the latter departments might consider whether statutory nuisance provisions should be used. Budget cuts and restructuring might have encouraged some changes to this situation, but the trend towards employing less qualified staff makes this monograph particularly timely.

1.07   The legislative background to this book is complicated. We start from the position that statutory nuisance has for many years been the only area of environmental health practice that explicitly addresses the problem of premises that pose a risk to health. Even when housing legislation introduced a definition of fitness (unfitness) in the 1950s, the standard of fitness did not mention health. It was down to the courts to determine what was meant by "reasonably suitable for occupation". Nowadays, EHOs have the HA 2004, which in Part 1 is specifically concerned about how housing affects the health and safety of occupiers. So the question can arise, when domestic premises are considered to be prejudicial or a risk to health, which provision should be used? We will examine, therefore, how EHOs should consider how that decision can best be made and, more importantly, the procedural matters that need to be borne in mind in making such a decision. For both approaches, best practice requires starting with the collection of good-quality evidence. And this requires a proper inspection of the property to be made and a thorough investigation of its problems – even though only a non-intrusive inspection can be undertaken.

1.08   This work is different from other works that have considered statutory nuisance alone in that it focuses on one particular aspect, that of domestic premises.[4] There will be other statutory nuisances that affect the residential setting, such as noise nuisance, which we also consider. Again, one must be careful to avoid mixing up regulatory approaches. Where a decision is made, for example, that noise emitted from premises amounts to a statutory nuisance, the local authority would be obliged to serve an abatement notice under s.80 of the EPA 1990 but could not serve a notice under the 2004 Act.

1.09   The statutory nuisance regime has the advantage that a "person aggrieved" by the nuisance, such as a tenant, may take their own action under s.82 of the EPA 1990. There is no equivalent route under the Housing Act. In this work, we will examine s.82 cases, some of which provide binding case law that EHPs have to bear in mind in carrying out their duties. Besides its capacity to deal with problems in the subject property, the statutory nuisance regime also allows enforcement action to be taken against the owner or occupier of a neighbouring property. If, for example, the source of dampness is the neighbour's leaking gutter, then an abatement notice can be served on that neighbour as the person responsible for the statutory nuisance. There is no equivalent power on the face of the HA 2004.[5]

1.10   Despite the relevance of current legislation for the issue of health and safety risks in housing, there remain significant gaps in provisions to protect tenants and occupiers. A recent report from the Law Schools of Bristol and Kent Universities,[6] following the Grenfell Tower tragedy, has suggested that the statutory nuisance provisions in s.82 of the EPA 1990 relating to housing conditions should be repealed. A comprehensive reform of housing law is needed, they argue, which requires a clear focus on the health and safety of occupiers and visitors. This suggestion and its implications will be discussed in more detail later in this work.

1.11   It is necessary to have an understanding of the historical development of the legislation. This is particularly true of statutory nuisance because this has implications for interpreting the scope of provisions that originated when the first Public Health Act was enacted in 1848. The first two of the main chapters look briefly at the historical development of the law on housing conditions and statutory nuisance. We also consider more recent forms of statutory nuisance, such as those caused by noise and artificial lighting. This historical treatment helps to explain the differences in the legislative regimes governing statutory nuisance and housing and why they should not be confused.

1.12   Chapter 4 considers more specifically the idea of "nuisance" as a common law tort or wrong, and this leads into the analysis of what is meant by "statutory nuisance". Here we discuss the distinction between the "prejudicial to health" and "nuisance" limbs of statutory nuisance in the EPA 1990.

1.13   The next two chapters discuss procedural and practice issues that arise from enforcing Part 1 of the Housing Act 2004 and Part III of the EPA 1990. These concentrate on dealing with problems associated with domestic premises and cover such topics as the investigation of complaints, the drafting and service of notices, defending appeals, and breach of notices.

1.14   In keeping with the tone of this work and trying to provide practical assistance to environmental health practitioners and others, Chapter 7 explores other remedies and powers that might be useful for addressing problems. Here we consider s.82 prosecutions by "persons aggrieved" under the EPA 1990 and the use of Community Protection Notices and injunctions made available by the Anti-social Behaviour, Crime and Policing Act 2014.

1.15   The penultimate chapter will look at how to resolve problems with residential property and will include examples of how things can go wrong and what can be done to avoid this. We also look at the differences (and similarities) in the powers available under the EPA 1990 and the Housing Act 2004. For example, where there is a problem of vermin in and around a property, the local authority has the option of using either of these Acts or even the Prevention of Damage by Pests Act 1949. So consideration needs to be given as to which power should be used as the basis for intervention.

1.16   The final chapter includes detailed case studies that illustrate the issues previously discussed and the dilemmas sometimes faced by local authority officers. Each case study provides a scenario, poses a number of questions, and finally provides some insight into possible solutions and responses. The aim here is to provide practical pointers as to how officers can decide on the best course of action when dealing with problems associated with domestic premises.

1.17   So this introduction explains the aims and structure of the monograph. We will also provide criticism of some current practices within local government and its approach to dealing with problems associated with residential property.

Notes

1 The MHCLG English Housing Survey Stock Condition Report reported that in 2016, of an estimated 23.7 million dwellings in England, 14.8 million (62%) were owner occupied, 4.9 million (20%) were in the private rented sector and 4.1 million (17%) were in the social rented sector.

2 Battersby SA, *Private Rented Sector Inspections and Local Housing Authority Staffing Supplementary Report for Karen Buck MP* (2018). Available at: www. sabattersby.co.uk/documents/Final_Staffing_Report_Master.pdf

3 Nicol S, Roys M, and Garrett H, *The Cost of Poor Housing to the NHS – Briefing Paper* (Watford: BRE Trust, 2015).

4 For a detailed analysis of statutory nuisance, see: Malcolm R and Pointing J, *Statutory Nuisance: Law and Practice*, 2nd edition (Oxford: OUP, 2011).

5 But see *Wood v Kingston upon Hull* [2017] EWCA Civ 364, in which Lord Justice Lewison said that: "(H)owever, the Deputy President's overall conclusion

that it was lawful for the Council to serve an improvement notice on Ms Peacock requiring her to carry out works to the ground floor flat (to address the hazard of fire in the flat above) was correct, although my reasoning has followed a different path".

6 Carr H, Cowan D, Kirton-Darling E, and Burtonshaw-Gunn E, *Closing the Gaps: Health and Safety at Home* (University of Bristol and University of Kent, 2017). Available at: www.bristol.ac.uk/media-library/sites/law/Closing%20 the%20gaps%20-%20Health%20and%20Safety%20at%20Home%20 (amended).pdf

2 Historical development of statutory nuisance

Historical background

2.01   The origins of statutory nuisance date back to the Industrial Revolution in Great Britain as a regime for improving the public health conditions of towns and cities. The earliest legislation was enacted in the late 1840s and was intended as a short-term response to combat serious diseases, in particular outbreaks of cholera then occurring in major towns and cities. At the time, this legislation was controversial, and opposition to it was self-serving and based on a *laissez-faire* philosophy. The *Economist* spoke for those opposed to "state interference" in voicing its opposition to the Public Health Bill of 1848:

> *The bill is but the beginning of an attempt, under the pretence of providing for the public health, to regulate by legislation . . . every business in every town of the empire, just as working in factories and mines has been lately taken in hand by legislation . . . [Such legislation] will check enterprise and self-exertion; it will beget reliance on boards instead of reliance on self; and by weakening the intellect and increasing the dependence of the people on government, will in the end more retard than promote the improvement of health.*[1]

The views of public health reformers and growth of public opinion in support of reform did, however, prevail in favour of state intervention once the Bill became law.

2.02   The concept of nuisance was central to the public health and sanitary legislation enacted in the 1840s and 1850s. The key legislation in this period was the Nuisances Removal and Diseases Prevention Act of 1855, which gave powers to local authorities, in England, to abate nuisances and deal with matters that were "injurious to health". It had become quite widely recognised by this time that public health and sanitary legislation that provided local authorities with powers enforced by state officials would be needed to improve urban living conditions. It had also become widely accepted that such legislation should be permanent if diseases and problems caused by insanitary housing were to be brought under control.

2.03   The statutory nuisance measures contained in the 1855 Act were subsequently consolidated in the 1875 Public Health Act. These statutory nuisance provisions formed only part of this pioneering Act, which laid the foundations for a modern industrial state. The 1875 Public Health Act was enacted by a Conservative government, though its preparation had been based on the work of the previous Liberal administration. Besides being supported by both parties, this legislation provided the platform for a variety of measures intended to improve living conditions in towns and cities. The Act contained provisions for building hospitals, mortuaries, and highways. It set out in a systematic way the powers and duties of local authorities. Besides the statutory nuisance provisions, the 1875 Act made regulations for sewers, drains, and water closets; rubbish disposal; cleansing of streets and ditches; provision of a clean water supply; and the regulation of cellar-dwellings and common lodging houses.

2.04   Some of the statutory nuisance provisions originating in nineteenth-century legislation have continued in essentially the same form into the next century: being consolidated in the 1936 Public Health Act and again in the 1990 Environmental Protection Act – the legislation now in force. These specific statutory nuisances are those resulting from the state of premises, the keeping of animals, or resulting from accumulations and deposits. These types of statutory nuisance were first enacted in the mid-nineteenth century, and the wording of these provisions has remained unaltered up to the present day. It is because of this long lineage that relatively recent, binding decisions of the High Court (and of the Court of Appeal and Supreme Court) interpreting the scope of these statutory nuisances often refer back to this early legislation. This is one reason why an understanding of the historical background to statutory nuisance is important for interpreting present-day law.

2.05   The aim of nineteenth-century statutory nuisance legislation was to encourage the improvement of living conditions, where they had deteriorated to such an extent as to cause nuisance or injury to health. The protection of the inhabitants of dwellings from industrial sources of pollution was also important, and this was why most forms of statutory nuisance – then and now – have applied both to residential property and to industrial, trade, or business premises.

2.06 As we have seen, the poor state of urban housing was of primary concern to public health reformers and legislators from the mid-nineteenth century. Sanitary legislation was enacted to deal with specific issues concerning dwellings: overcrowding, serious disrepair, lack of a clean water supply, lack of adequate drainage, and poor facilities for the removal of human and animal excrement and rubbish.[2] For reformers, the risks were from diseases caused by overcrowding, dampness, and accumulations of filth. The state of housing – poor standards of building to high densities, poor internal arrangement and lack of facilities, the deterioration of dwellings due to overcrowding and the neglect of landlords to maintain them – was at the top of the political agenda by the 1870s. The state of housing has remained in this position for most of the twentieth and twenty-first centuries.

The Environmental Protection Act 1990, Part III

2.07 The statutory nuisance legislation now in force is set down in Part III of the Environmental Protection Act 1990 (EPA 1990). The Act applies to England and Wales as well as to Scotland (with some variations). In Northern Ireland, the Clean Neighbourhoods and Environment Act (Northern Ireland) 2011 applies.

2.08 The law of statutory nuisance is concerned with a wide range of matters. These include: atmospheric pollution, sanitary nuisances mainly affecting residential property, and more recent types of nuisance such as noise and light pollution. Thus, the list of statutory nuisances has been added to over the years. Those currently in effect are set down in s.79(1) of the EPA 1990. **Table 2.1** applies to England and Wales. The list for Scotland differs in respect of statutory nuisances involving land covered by water, insects, and artificial light. Statutory nuisances in Northern Ireland are set out in s.63 of the Clean Neighbourhoods and Environment Act (Northern Ireland) 2011.

2.09 Any of the preceding statutory nuisances will result either because they are nuisances at common law or because they are prejudicial to health.[3] Linking a particular statutory nuisance to one of these limbs is a basic, good practice requirement. An investigating officer has the responsibility for deciding, on behalf of the local authority, whether the requirements of s.80 of the EPA 1990 are met. He or she must be "satisfied that a statutory nuisance exists, or is likely to occur or recur" before an abatement notice can be served on the person responsible. The various types of statutory nuisance that can apply to residential property will next be considered.

Table 2.1 List of statutory nuisances: section 79(1) Environmental Health Act 1990
(as amended)

(a)	any premises in such a state as to be prejudicial to health or a nuisance;
(b)	smoke emitted from premises so as to be prejudicial to health or a nuisance;
(c)	fumes or gases emitted from premises so as to be prejudicial to health or a nuisance;
(d)	any dust, steam, smell or other effluvia arising on industrial, trade or business premises and being prejudicial to health or a nuisance;
(e)	any accumulation or deposit which is prejudicial to health or a nuisance;
(f)	any animal kept in such a place or manner as to be prejudicial to health or a nuisance;
(fa)	any insects emanating from relevant industrial, trade or business premises and being prejudicial to health or a nuisance;
(fb)	artificial light emitted from premises so as to be prejudicial to health or a nuisance;
(g)	noise emitted from premises so as to be prejudicial to health or a nuisance;
(ga)	noise that is prejudicial to health or a nuisance and is emitted from or caused by a vehicle, machinery or equipment in a street or in Scotland, road;
(h)	any other matter declared by any enactment to be a statutory nuisance.

State of the premises: s. 79(1)(a)

2.10   Section 79(1)(a) EPA 1990 applies to a dwelling that has fallen into such a state that it amounts to a risk to the health of its occupants. The type of health risk associated with this provision must be related to infectious or contagious diseases, not personal injury.[4] Premises will also come within the scope of this provision if they are in such a state as to cause a nuisance and/or a health risk to neighbouring property. Problems resulting from obsolete or bad design, a lack of facilities, or the poor layout of rooms do not come within the scope of this provision.[5] The lack of adequate sound insulation cannot render the premises prejudicial to health.[6]

Atmospheric emissions

2.11   Types of statutory nuisance in the EPA 1990 arise from emissions **from** premises, namely: smoke – s.79(1)(b) and fumes or gases – s.79(1)(c). The wording of these provisions implies that neighbouring property, rather than the source property, needs to be affected for them to be applicable.

Dust, steam, smell, or other effluvia: s.79(1)(d)

2.12 Statutory nuisances arising **on** premises of dust, steam, smell, or other effluvia come within s.79(1)(d). It should be noted that s.79(1)(d) only applies to emissions arising on industrial, trade, or business premises and not on residential premises. Cooking smells – or any of these emissions in s.79(1)(d) – from domestic premises do not come within the scope of the provision. Of course, residential property may be affected by this type of statutory nuisance (under both its limbs) where the emissions originate from industrial, trade, or business premises.

2.13 The use of "on" rather than "from" in s.79(1)(d) implies that if the emissions are prejudicial to health to those working or visiting the premises, then the case is actionable as a statutory nuisance. However, using the Health and Safety at Work Act 1974 as the basis for regulation may be more appropriate than the EPA 1990. Health and safety legislation imposes a general duty of care on employers and on those in control of businesses to protect the health and safety of employees and other persons associated with the activity of the business. Section 5 of the Health and Safety at Work Act 1974 sets out a duty of care in regard to harmful emissions into the atmosphere imposed on persons in control of certain types of premises.

2.14 If the activity of the business consists of a "prescribed process", then it is regulated by a different regime than statutory nuisance or the Health and Safety at Work Act 1974. Prescribed processes come within the scope of Part I of the EPA 1990, which is an entirely separate regulatory system from the statutory nuisance provisions in Part III.

Smoke: s.79(1)(b)

2.15 "Smoke" is defined in s.79(7) EPA 1990 to include "soot, ash or gritty particles emitted in smoke". As we have seen, there must be an emission from premises. As the definition of premises in the Act includes land, this type of statutory nuisance includes smoke from bonfires in gardens as well as emissions from buildings.[7]

2.16 A number of exclusions to the smoke nuisances in s.79(1)(b) apply in order to avoid conflict with other legislation. Emissions of "dark smoke" from industrial or trade premises are excluded from coming within the scope of statutory nuisance by s.79(3) EPA 1990. Section 1 of the Clean Air Act 1993 prohibits "dark smoke" being emitted from a chimney of any building. This legislation should therefore be used for regulating dark smoke emissions from chimneys.

2.17   With regard to residential property, the smoke nuisance provision of s.79(1)(b) EPA 1990 is limited to smoke emitted from a fire or grate outside of a smoke control area. Emissions of smoke from chimneys within a smoke control area are regulated by s.20 of the Clean Air Act 1993. Smoke leaking from defects in the structure of the building rather than from a chimney could amount to a statutory nuisance under s.79(1)(b).

Fumes or gases: s.79(1)(c)

2.18   Fumes or gases emitted from premises can amount to a statutory nuisance under s.79(1)(c) EPA 1990. As with smoke nuisances, the use of the word "from" in the statute implies that the provision is only actionable where neighbouring property is affected. This provision applies only to emissions from private dwellings. It originated in 1990 to reflect the reality that gas central heating had become the norm for residential property. So this type of statutory nuisance applies where the exiting fumes or gases from a central heating plant – even where it conforms to the gas regulations – cannot dissipate because of the physical layout of the buildings. This provision does not apply to cooking smells – whether foul or not – or to smoke nuisances. It should not be used to regulate emissions from barbeques.

Any accumulations or deposit: s.79(1)(e)

2.19   The regulation of accumulations and deposits first became a statutory nuisance – under the nuisance and/or health limbs – in 1855. It remains the same in its current form: s.79(1)(e) EPA 1990. For the health limb to apply, the accumulation or deposit has to involve "something which produces a threat to health in the sense of a threat of disease, vermin or the like".[8]

2.20   There is no definition in the EPA 1990 of "accumulation or deposit". The *Oxford English Dictionary Online* defines "accumulation" as "an accumulated mass; a heap, pile, or quantity formed by successive additions". "Deposit" is defined as "something deposited, laid or thrown down; a mass or layer of matter that has subsided or been precipitated from a fluid medium, or has collected in one place by any natural process".

2.21   A person who carries out an action causing an accumulation or deposit to arise clearly comes within the scope of this statutory nuisance. Persons can also be held responsible if they allow an accumulation or deposit to take place on their land. They may also be held liable for failing to abate the statutory nuisance resulting from a natural process leaving an accumulation or deposit on their land.[9]

2.22 A very wide range of circumstances is covered by the phrase "any accumulation or deposit". Decided case law includes such matters as:

- an accumulation of building rubble on a demolition site;[10]
- a deposit of sewage and sewage-related material on a beach;[11]
- an accumulation of seaweed in a harbour;[12]
- a pile of garden manure which gave off smells and attracted flies;[13]
- an accumulation of dung;[14]
- refuse deposited against the front boundary wall of a property;[15]
- railway trucks standing at a station and loaded with manure.[16]

2.23 Large-scale accumulations or deposits resulting from industrial processes are likely to be controlled by other regulatory systems. Section 79(10) EPA 1990 imposes a block on a local authority instituting summary proceedings under the statutory nuisance regime for dealing with accumulations or deposits in certain circumstances. Thus, "prescribed processes", coming within the scope of Part I EPA 1990, are regulated under separate provisions. In addition, the management of waste products comes within a separate regime, set down in Part II EPA 1990.

Keeping of animals: s.79(1)(f)

2.24 The keeping of animals can amount to a statutory nuisance under s.79(1)(f) EPA 1990. This type of statutory nuisance focuses on the premises, on the place where an animal is kept, or on the way it is kept. It does not extend to the activities of an animal off the premises, such as livestock trespassing and causing damage on another's land or pest damage.[17] The suitability of the premises where animals are kept and the conditions of their keeping are what this provision is aimed at. A key question is whether anything defective or insanitary about the premises causes nuisance or prejudice to health to arise from the keeping of animals.[18]

2.25 Defective fencing, allowing a large number of cats to stray onto neighbouring premises to deposit faeces, has been held to amount to statutory nuisance.[19] The straying of one or two cats in this way, however, might be considered to fall below the threshold for nuisance and to be insufficient to amount to a risk to health.

2.26   Feral or wild pigeons – more particularly, their faeces – can cause a private or a public nuisance where such birds roost on the roofs and in the eaves of buildings and underneath bridges. The Public Health Act 1961, s.74 empowers local authorities to cull house doves, pigeons, starlings, or sparrows where sufficient numbers cause annoyance, damage, or nuisance. Feral birds cannot be said to be "kept" by the owners of buildings or other structures, so s.79(1)(f) of the EPA 1990 ought not to be used. The local authority could consider dealing with the matter as coming within the scope of "accumulations or deposits" under s.79(1)(e) of the EPA 1990.

2.27   Section 79(1)(f) of the EPA 1990 has been interpreted in a restricted way by the courts. It has been held not to include noise nuisance from animals kept on premises,[20] and local authorities should consider using the noise provision in s.79(1)(g) instead.

Insects: s.79(1)(fa)

2.28   Insects emanating from relevant industrial, trade or business premises became a statutory nuisance for England and Wales in 2006.[21] Premises where animals are kept and sewage treatment works have been notable among the premises giving rise to nuisances from insects.[22] Other problem areas include landfill and waste treatment sites, stagnant areas of water, and abattoirs. Agricultural land and domestic premises are excluded from this provision (but not in Scotland).

Artificial light: s.79(1)(fb)

2.29   Artificial light emitted from premises became a statutory nuisance for England and Wales in 2006.[23] There are a number of exempted premises, such as transportation facilities and prisons.[24] Artificial light emitted from domestic premises – from such sources as security and decorative lighting – and causing a nuisance to neighbours was a primary reason for the government introducing this measure.[25]

Noise: s.79(1)(g)

2.30   Noise nuisance first became a statutory nuisance in the UK (but not in Northern Ireland) with the Noise Abatement Act 1960. Later changes were made by the Control of Pollution 1974. Today, noise from premises causing a nuisance or being prejudicial to health is a statutory nuisance throughout the UK, under s.79(1)(g) EPA 1990.[26]

2.31 Noise can become a nuisance in many circumstances, but only rarely will it come within the scope of the prejudicial to health limb of statutory nuisance. The premises from which the noise is emitted can be from industrial, trade, or business premises, in which case a "best practicable means" defence is available under the EPA 1990, s.80(7). "Premises" does not include a street or highway. However, noise "emitted from or caused by a vehicle, machinery or equipment in a street" may be actionable under a separate provision of the EPA 1990: s.79(1)(ga).

2.32 Complaints about noise form the majority of nuisance complaints to local authorities.[27] Inadequate sound insulation between residential properties exacerbates the problem, and the everyday sounds of ordinary living may cause considerable annoyance and nuisance to neighbours. This will often be the case with older flats and house conversions in both the private and social housing sectors.

2.33 Domestic noise nuisance – as with all forms of nuisance – is subject to the test of "reasonable user" or the principle of give and take. Unless there is an unreasonable element, normal, everyday noise will not constitute a statutory nuisance.[28]

2.34 Domestic noise forms an important part of the government's anti-social behaviour agenda. Ways of dealing with anti-social or "nuisance neighbours" form the subject of guidance to local authorities from the Chartered Institute of Environmental Health.[29]

Statutory nuisances declared by any other enactment: s.79(1)(h)

2.35 Section 79(1)(h) of the EPA 1990 incorporates statutory nuisances remaining in force from the Public Health Act 1936. This Act applies to England and Wales, and different statutory provisions apply in Scotland and in Northern Ireland. Public Health Act statutory nuisances affecting residential property include those arising from:

- *any pond, pool, ditch, gutter or watercourse which is so foul or in such a state as to be prejudicial to health or a nuisance;*[30]

- *any well, tank, cistern, or water-butt used for the supply of water for domestic purposes which is so placed, constructed or kept as to render the water therein liable to contamination prejudicial to health;*[31]
- *a tent, van, shed or similar structure used for human habitation –*

    a   *which is in such a state, or so overcrowded as to be prejudicial to the health of the inmates; or*

    b   *the use of which, by reason of the absence of proper sanitary accommodation or otherwise, gives rise, whether on the site or on other land, to a nuisance or to conditions prejudicial to health.*[32]

2.36   The Building Act 1984 makes provision for dealing with statutory nuisances arising from the sanitary element of the building structure. Section 59 of the Act applies where satisfactory provision has not been made regarding the drainage of a building or where there is defective plant, such as a cesspool, private sewer, drain, etc. Additionally, section 59 provides:

if it appears to a local authority that in the case of a building that –
. . .

    c   *a cesspool or other such work or appliance . . . provided for the building is in such a condition as to be prejudicial to health or a nuisance, or*

    d   *a cesspool, private sewer or drain formerly used for the drainage of the building, but no longer used for it, is prejudicial to health or a nuisance, they shall by notice require the owner of the building [to make good those defects].*

2.37   The Public Health Act 1936 contains a separate provision to deal with defective closets in buildings which, though capable of repair, are in such a state as to be prejudicial to health or a nuisance. The local authority "shall by notice require the owner or the occupier of the building to execute such works, or to take such steps by cleansing the closets or otherwise, as may be necessary".[33]

Notes

1   *Economist*, 20 May 1848, 565–566.
2   Burnett J, *A Social History of Housing, 1815–1985* (London: Routledge, 1991).
3   *National Coal Board v Neath BC (or Thorne)* [1976] 2 All ER 478.
4   *R v Bristol City Council, ex p Everett* [1999] 1 WLR 1170.
5   *Birmingham City Council v Oakley* [2001] 1 All ER 385.

6 *R (on the application of Vella) v Lambeth London Borough Council* [2005] EWHC 2473 (Admin).
7 *Griffiths v Pembrokeshire County Council* [2000] Env LR 622.
8 *Coventry City Council v Cartwright* [1975] 1 WLR 845, 849.
9 EPA 1990, s.79(7).
10 *Coventry City Council v Cartwright* [1975] 1 WLR 845.
11 *R v Carrick DC, ex p Shelley* [1996] Env LR 273.
12 *Margate Pier and Harbour (Proprietors Co) v Margate Town Council* [1869] 33 JP 437.
13 *Bland v Yates* [1914] 58 SJ 612.
14 *Smith v Waghorn* [1863] 27 JP 744.
15 *Stanley v London Borough of Ealing* [2000] 32 HLR 745.
16 *London, Brighton & South Coast Railway v Haywards Heath UDC* [1899] 86 LT 266.
17 Local authorities are empowered under the Prevention of Damage by Pests Act 1949, Part I to destroy rats and mice and to require owners to take treatment measures or to carry out repairs to property to prevent damage and nuisance from these pests.
18 *Galer v Morrissey* [1955] 1 All ER 380.
19 *R v Walden-Jones, ex p Coton* [1963] Crim LR 839.
20 *Galer v Morrissey* [1955] 1 All ER 380.
21 Clean Neighbourhoods and Environment Act 2005, s.101. In Northern Ireland, a similar provision was included in the Clean Neighbourhoods and Environment Act (Northern Ireland) 2011. In Scotland, a similar provision in the Public Health (Scotland) Act 2008, s.109 applies to all types of premises.
22 *Dobson v Thames Water Utilities Ltd* [2009] EWCA Civ 28.
23 Clean Neighbourhoods and Environment Act 2005, s.102. In Northern Ireland, a similar provision was included in the Clean Neighbourhoods and Environment Act (Northern Ireland) 2011. In Scotland, a wider provision in the Public Health (Scotland) Act 2008 includes "artificial light emitted from premises or any stationary object".
24 EPA 1990, s.79(5B).
25 *Hansard*, 10 January 2008, col 731W, Written Answer.
26 The noise nuisance provisions in Northern Ireland are the same, made by the Clean Neighbourhoods and Environment Act (Northern Ireland) 2011, s.63(1)(i).
27 Statistics compiled by the Chartered Institute of Environmental Health suggest that over 70% of all noise complaints concern domestic noise.
28 *Baxter v Camden London Borough Council (No.2)* [2001] 1 AC 1.
29 *Guidance on the Use of Community Protection Notices under Part 5 of the Anti-social Behaviour, Crime and Policing Act 2014* (CIEH, November 2017). Available at: www.cieh.org/media/1238/guidance-on-the-use-of-community-protection-notices.pdf
30 Public Health Act 1936, s.259(1)(a). A similar provision to s.259(1)(a) is provided for Northern Ireland by s.63(1)(k) of the Clean Neighbourhoods and Environment Act (Northern Ireland) 2011. For Scotland, a much wider provision is provided by s.79(1)(ea) of the EPA 1990: "any water covering land or land covered with water which is in such a state as to be prejudicial to health or a nuisance".
31 *Ibid.*, s.141.

32 *Ibid.*, s.268(2). A much wider provision is available in Northern Ireland. Section 63(1)(m) of the Clean Neighbourhoods and Environment Act (Northern Ireland) 2011 provides that: "any private dwelling so overcrowded as to be prejudicial to health of those living there or a nuisance" shall constitute a statutory nuisance.

33 *Ibid.*, s.45.

3 Development of the law on housing conditions

Public health and housing in the nineteenth century

3.01   As discussed in Chapter 2, much of the original legislation dealing with poor housing conditions emanated from sanitary or public
health legislation. Such legislation became necessary as a result of
the great economic, social, and environmental changes taking place
from the end of the eighteenth century and into the nineteenth century. There was increasing urbanisation and industrialisation, resulting in the movement of people into the towns where they often
lived in crowded, sprawling, and insanitary settlements. While the
"miasma" theory – that foul air caused diseases we now know to be
caused by waterborne bacteria – might have been wrong scientifi-
cally, it did mean that those in more powerful positions in society
and higher up the social scale felt that something had to be done
about the squalor of the slums and places where the working classes
were crowded together. Many reformers were motivated to call for
changes in approach, particularly when the effects of the insanitary
conditions spread to the middle and upper classes and because the
causes of such diseases as cholera and typhoid were becoming more
clearly identified.

3.02   The first "housing measures" (rather than direct public health or sanitary legislation) were the Common Lodging Houses Act 1851 and
Labouring Classes Lodging Act 1851. The Public Health Act of 1848
had empowered the local board of health to make by-laws to regulate common lodging houses in the interests of public health. This
included fixing a maximum number of lodgers permitted to sleep
in each house, promoting cleanliness and ventilation, providing for
inspection visits and ensuring the segregation of the sexes. These
powers were extended in the Common Lodging Houses Act of 1851.
The two Acts of 1851 are often referred to as the "Shaftsbury Acts"

(after the Earl of Shaftsbury). These Acts also made it a requirement for the authorities to keep a register of owners of lodging houses and of the houses themselves. They required lodging house proprietors to notify the local authority if any case of contagious or infectious disease occurred, so perhaps these Acts were both a "housing" and a "public health" measure.

3.03   The second of these two Acts gave boroughs and vestries the power to raise funds via local rates and gave the Public Works Loan Commissioners powers to build lodging houses for unmarried working (as opposed to unemployed) people. At that time, the totally destitute would be destined for the workhouse, but those who had some income could access the common lodging house. The difference from the workhouse was that there was no requirement to carry out work whilst lodging in the common lodging house. In a common lodging house, it was not unusual for the fee to cover only a share of a bed, so that two or even three people could be using the same bed on a shift basis, popularly known at the time as "box and cox".

3.04   The 1855 Nuisances Removal Act allowed action against overcrowding to be taken by the local authority to abate nuisance.[1] It was overcrowding that led to night inspections. There was much discussion at the time of the minimum space needed for healthy living. It has been suggested that the figure settled on in the Sanitary Act of 1866 was 300 cubic feet per person, with children counting as half persons and cows as five person-equivalents.[2] This was at a time when Dr Duncan, the first Medical Officer of Health[3] refers to the criteria used by the Inspectors of Prisons, who recommended not less than 1000 cubic feet for every prisoner, that is 28.3 cubic metres. (For comparison, a room of 6.5 square metres with an average ceiling height would have a space of 15.6 cubic metres (551 cubic feet).)

3.05   A variety of other measures were legislated during the mid-nineteenth century that gave local authorities or boards powers to provide housing for the working classes or to deal with insanitary or unfit housing. During this period, what made a dwelling unfit was not defined in legislation. The Labouring Classes Dwellings Act 1866 allowed the Public Works Loan Commission to loan money to fund the construction of housing for the labouring classes. The Artisans and Labourers Dwellings Act 1868 (Torrens Act) required the Officer of Health to report as to the condition of streets. If in any local authority area to which this Act applied (set out in a schedule), the Officer of Health (defined as including the Medical Officer of Health and Sanitary Inspector) found that any premises were in a "condition or state dangerous to health so as to be unfit for human habitation", the Officer had a duty to report this to the local authority. The authority then prepared a report to be given to the owner, plus a plan and specification of required works. Following a "time and place" meeting to consider the owner's views and any objections, the authority had to make an order requiring the owner to carry out those works.

3.06   The Artisans and Labourers Dwellings Improvement Act 1875 (Cross Act) was the brainchild of Richard Cross, the Home Secretary in Disraeli's second government. This allowed local authorities to buy up areas of slum dwellings in order to clear and then rebuild them – really the first slum clearance legislation. The Artisans and Labourers Dwellings Improvement Act 1879 further developed and amended the 1875 Act so that local authorities could compulsorily purchase dwellings that were "unfit for human habitation". The aim was for local authorities to build new houses to be let, but problems of rehousing tenants displaced by development at affordable rents continued. The Artisans Dwellings Act 1882 extended the provisions of the 1875 and 1879 Acts, but the focus remained on clearing slum areas.

3.07   The Housing of the Working Classes Acts 1885 and 1890 consolidated much of the previous housing legislation; and the 1890 Act remained the principal housing legislation until 1925. The 1885 Act followed a Royal Commission report on the reasons for the lack of decent housing available for the working classes. This Act laid down that every local authority entrusted with the execution of laws relating to public health must enforce them so as to secure the proper sanitary condition of all premises within their district. It also empowered local authorities to make by-laws in respect of houses let in lodgings. The 1890 Act included simplified procedures for dealing with unfit housing and empowered local authorities to build council houses using money from the rates. It also placed a duty on medical officers of health to report unfit houses and slum areas to their local authorities.

The twentieth century and healthy housing interventions

3.08   Separation of housing and sanitary legislation became more evident in the twentieth century and particularly after the First World War. During the last decade of the nineteenth century, the "garden city" movement became influential. Ebenezer Howard had developed new principles of town layout and architectural design to create spacious, tree-lined avenues of houses for working people, embodying the best features of both town and countryside. The Housing and Town

Planning Act 1909 and the Housing and Town Planning Act 1919 (Addison Act) were the first clear examples of the separation of sanitary legislation from housing law.

3.09   It was the 1909 Act which sought to prevent the building of "back-to-back" houses. This Act also required local authorities to introduce systems of town planning and homes had to be built to certain standards. It was the duty of every local authority – as in the Housing of the Working Classes Act 1890 (the principal Act at the time) – to consider the needs of their area with respect to the provision of houses for the working classes and to prepare and submit to the Local Government Board a scheme for the exercise of their powers. Under the 1909 Act, if the owner of any house suitable for occupation by persons of the working classes failed to make and keep such a house in all respects reasonably fit for human habitation (not defined), then the local authority could serve a notice upon the owner. This notice could require the owner – within a reasonable time, being not less than twenty-one days, specified in the notice – to execute such works as may be necessary to make the house in all respects reasonably fit for human habitation. If the house was not capable, without reconstruction, of being rendered fit for human habitation, the owner could, within twenty-one days of receipt of the notice, declare in writing his intention of closing the house for human habitation, and then a closing order would be deemed to have become operative.

3.10   After the 1919 Addison Act, councils came to be the main providers of housing for the working classes, as they began to plan and implement their post-war housing programmes. Housing committees were set up, working largely from recommendations from the central government's advisory committee (the Tudor Walters Committee), and were encouraged to build through the provision of generous subsidies. The subsidy arrangements shared the costs of this new housing among the tenants, local ratepayers, and central government (the Treasury).

The development of standards for existing housing

3.11   In 1919, the Ministry of Health took over the powers and duties of the Local Government Board and the National Health Insurance Commissions for England and Wales. It was only then, in the *Manual on Unfit Houses and Unhealthy Areas*, that any thought was given to defining "unfitness". The fitness standard proposed was as follows:

A fit house should be:-

1   *free from serious dampness*
2   *satisfactorily lighted and ventilated;*
3   *properly drained and provided with adequate sanitary conveniences and with a sink and suitable arrangements for disposing of slop water; and*
4   *in good general repair;*
    and should have:
5   *a satisfactory water supply;*
6   *adequate washing accommodation;*
7   *adequate facilities for preparing and cooking food; and*
8   *a well-ventilated food store.*

This standard was not incorporated into legislation, and it was some decades before any standard was defined in legislation.

3.12   The Housing (Financial Provisions) Act 1924 (Wheatley Act) was the brainchild of the Health Minister, John Wheatley, who was the Health Secretary at the time. Housing was still being seen as a public health issue at this time. Wheatley sought to draft a piece of legislation to remedy the existing social housing crisis, so the main thrust of housing legislation should be to clear slums and, more particularly, to increase provision of decent affordable housing. This Act allowed central government to provide increased subsidies to build public housing and extended the period over which it could be paid for. This measure provided homes at affordable rents for low-income families as well as boosting the construction industry. It was during this period that many of the large-scale council estates, such as can be seen today in Liverpool and Birmingham, were built on greenfield sites.

3.13   The Housing (Rural Workers) Act 1926 permitted rural councils to submit schemes for assistance to improve conditions of the homes of rural workers. This was the first time that rural councils could benefit from central government grants. No assistance could be given under the Act unless the local authority were satisfied that the dwelling would, after the completion of the works, "be in all respects fit for habitation as a dwelling by persons of the working class".[4] The use of this provision was wholly discretionary, and there was no requirement for local authorities to provide such assistance.

3.14   The Housing Act 1930 (often known as the Greenwood Act, after Arthur Greenwood the then Housing Minister) made further provisions for Clearance Areas – including compulsory purchase – and for the improvement of unhealthy areas. In part, this was necessary because, while local authorities had had the powers to clear areas of poor housing, many had not made full use of their powers. The Act included a duty imposed on local authorities to review housing conditions in their areas and to "frame proposals", so that each had to submit a programme of building and demolition aimed at eliminating slums in their districts. The Housing Act 1930 thus provided greater impetus for mass slum clearance, which enabled councils, once the Act came into force, to demolish poor-quality housing and replace it with new-build homes on a larger scale. The Housing Act 1935 gave further impetus to slum clearance, leading to the aspiration that the slums would be eradicated within a matter of years. But then the Second World War intervened to dash such hopes.

3.15   The Housing Act 1949 was the first time that councils had to take account of the housing needs of all and not just those of the "working classes". It allowed local authorities to acquire homes for improvement or conversion and provided them with substantial Exchequer grants. The Act removed the restriction imposed upon local authorities by previous housing legislation which limited them to providing housing for working-class people only. This change allowed local authorities to develop mixed estates of houses of more varied types and sizes, thereby attracting all income groups. In addition, housing improvement grants for private landlords and owner occupiers were introduced under the Act. This piece of housing legislation reflected a policy which sought to help owner occupiers, as local authorities were to direct these grants towards bringing properties up to a sixteen-point standard. Grants were also made available to landlords to provide the basic amenities.

3.16   The Housing Rents and Repairs Act 1954 amended housing law and the exercise of certain powers relating to land. It also made provisions for rent control. The Act included provisions for the clearance and redevelopment of areas of unfit housing and for securing or promoting the reconditioning and maintenance of houses via improvement grants. Grants were seen as a means of "buying time", which facilitated the provision of better accommodation until such time as the properties could be demolished and replaced.

3.17   The Housing Rents and Repairs Act 1954 required local authorities to survey all houses in their district to determine which were unfit. For the first time, a fitness standard was defined in legislation. Section 4 of the Housing Act 1957 subsequently incorporated this standard of fitness, which remained the standard for the next thirty years, with only minor changes being made until 1989. Section 4 stated that:

In determining for any of the purposes of this Act whether a house is unfit for human habitation, regard shall be had to its condition in respect of the following matters, that is to say –

a repair;
b stability;
c freedom from damp;
d natural lighting;
e ventilation;
f water supply;
g drainage and sanitary conveniences;
h facilities for storage, preparation, and cooking of food and for the disposal of waste water;

[and the house was] deemed to be unfit for human habitation if and only if it is so far defective in one or more of the said matters that it is not reasonably suitable for occupation in that condition.

3.18 The Housing Act 1957 permitted local authorities to require the "repair" of unfit houses which could be made fit at "reasonable expense" – so there was no longer an assumption that unfitness should lead to demolition. While much emphasis was still being placed on areas needing slum clearance and building new homes, new powers were included to deal with poor housing conditions and disrepair on an individual basis, including closing and Demolition Orders. Section 5 continued the prohibition on the construction of back-to-back houses. This provision was to be repealed in the 1980s as part of the deregulatory drive started under the government of Mrs Thatcher. The 1957 Act also gave a power for local authorities to acquire land for the provision of accommodation. The Housing (Financial Provisions) Act 1958 introduced further changes to the improvement grant system. This was followed by the House Purchase and Housing Act 1959, which placed a duty on local authorities to provide grant assistance to secure the provision of the standard amenities: the standard grant.

3.19 Although by 1969 the power to provide financial assistance had existed for some time, the Housing Act of that year was much concerned with promoting the improvement of existing housing. This indicated a change in policy in favour of retaining more existing housing rather than clearance and replacement, particularly on an area basis rather than individually. The first part of the Act was concerned with: improvement grants, standard grants for the provision of the basic amenities and some repairs, and special grants to bring houses in multiple occupation up to standard. The Act also introduced the concept of General Improvement Areas. This area approach was seen as appropriate where "living conditions in the area ought to be improved by the improvement of the amenities of the area or of dwellings therein or both". The fitness standard was amended to include "internal arrangement" and omit "storage" from the criterion on food preparation etc.

3.20   The 1969 Act also introduced s.9(1A) into the 1957 Act to enable local authorities to require works to be carried out to houses, which, although not unfit, were in substantial disrepair. The Housing Act 1974 further developed the area approach with the introduction of Housing Action Areas, as well as a revised system of improvement grants. The Act also provided special grants for HMOs and made the standard grant the intermediate grant with works of repair included. Additionally, local authorities were given new compulsory improvement powers. This legislation initiated the era of "area improvement" and gradual urban renewal or regeneration. The 1980 Housing Act further amended the powers of local authorities by introducing ss.9(1B) and 9(1C) into the 1957 Act. This allowed local authorities to deal with a house in a "state of disrepair that, although it is not unfit for human habitation, the condition of the house is such as to interfere materially with the personal comfort of the occupying tenant". The local authority could also act on the representation (complaint) of the occupying tenant.

3.21   The Housing Act 1985 consolidated much of the existing housing legislation, so that the standard of fitness became s.604 in the 1985 Act. Shortly afterwards, the Local Government and Housing Act 1989 contained the first major update of the fitness standard since 1957. It included the basic amenities and space heating for the first time, along with mandatory grants for owner occupiers of unfit houses, with no upper limit to grants, although subject to means testing. This standard of fitness replaced a broad, cumulative assessment with a requirement that a dwelling must fail one or more of the prescribed criteria.[5] The 1989 Act was also accompanied by a Government Circular that set out in detail, for the first time, extensive guidance on the interpretation of the fitness standard and emphasised the health effects of any failures in meeting the criteria.

Towards the twenty-first century

3.22   With the 1989 fitness standard now being linked to a mandatory grant regime, the government set up arrangements for monitoring how this revised fitness standard was being interpreted. It was found that there were wide variations in interpreting the standard and that the existence of mandatory, if means tested, grants for owner occupiers meant that some substantial grants were being made which influenced how the standard was being interpreted. One particular problem concerned what was meant by "reasonably suitable for occupation".[6] The report prepared for the Department of the Environment also pointed out that some of the major issues affecting the risks to health and safety in dwellings were not being addressed. For example, for space heating, the guidance suggested that a single electric socket would suffice. This led to a further report, prepared by Warwick Law School on controlling minimum standards in existing housing.[7] This reported that the "role of the Housing Fitness Standard has changed in recent years. Originally an intervention standard concerned with public health and safety issues, it is both an intervention and improvement standard". Even at the "intervention" level, the term "not reasonably suitable for occupation" was being interpreted very differently around the country.[8]

3.23   The Housing Grants Construction and Regeneration Act 1996 amended the grants regime further, making renovation grants for unfit owner-occupied houses no longer mandatory. It did introduce "deferred action notices" that the local housing authority could serve when it was satisfied that a dwelling-house or house in multiple occupation (HMO) was unfit for human habitation but were also satisfied that serving a deferred action notice would be the most satisfactory course of action. In effect, the local authority was no longer under a duty to ensure that an unfit dwelling was made fit for human habitation. A deferred action notice was a notice merely stating that a dwelling was unfit, listing the works necessary to make it fit, and also listing the other courses of action that were available to the authority. Meanwhile, of course, the occupier (tenant) remained living in the unfit property.

3.24   As a result of research carried out during the 1990s, following the Local Government and Housing Act 1989, a new approach to assessing housing conditions was being developed. This is based very much on the risks to health and safety arising from the conditions and deficiencies identified – so we may have come full circle. The Housing Act 2004 introduced the concept of Category 1 and Category 2 hazards. How these hazards were to be determined was by using the Housing Health and Safety Rating System (HHSRS). Much of this monograph considers the practical issues relating to the HHSRS and the powers set down in Part 1 of the 2004 Act. These powers reflect many of those introduced over the decades and previously set out, so that, for example, the Hazard Awareness Notice in the 2004 Act can be seen as a descendant of the deferred action notice in the 1996 Act.

3.25 Of relevance to the legislative changes considered in this chapter and the issues addressed in later chapters is the changing nature of tenure patterns. Until the early 1990s, the story of private renting was one of long-term decline: from representing 76% of households (in England and Wales) in 1918 to a low point of just 9% in 1991. For several decades up to the 1980s, it was generally thought that the private rented sector would be reduced to a rump – providing accommodation only at the very top and the very bottom (often HMOs) of the housing market. This belief prevailed, in part, because the decline in private renting corresponded with the huge rise, over the century, in home ownership and increased social renting.[9]

3.26 Change was initiated during the 1980s when the "right to buy" legislation was enacted, as well as measures weakening security of tenure for private tenants. Since 1996–97, the proportion of private rented sector households has doubled, and the overall size of this sector has increased from 2.1 million households in 1996–97 to 4.7 million in 2016–17.[10] The private rented sector grew between 1996–97 and 2006–07, but growth accelerated after 2006–07, with over 2 million additional households being added. This change came about for a number of reasons: a favourable tax system, the lack of availability of council and housing association accommodation, and the growth of buy-to-let loans for landlords. Letting to private tenants became attractive as the prevailing low interest rates were a result of the financial crisis, and investing in residential property gave a better return than other forms of investment.

Notes

1 Overcrowding in dwellings as a statutory nuisance was repealed by the Public Health Act 1936. The Act did not apply to Northern Ireland, and overcrowding in private dwellings remains a statutory nuisance there, in s.63(1)((m) Clean Neighbourhoods and Environment Act (Northern Ireland) 2011.
2 Hamlin C, Nuisances and Community in Mid-Victorian England: The Attractions of Inspection. *Social History* Vol. 38, No. 3 (2013), 346–379, https://doi.org/10.1080/03071022.2013.817061
3 Battersby SA, Duncan of Liverpool: The First Medical Officer of Health, in: *Pioneers in Public Health*, Stewart J (Ed) (London: Routledge, 2017).
4 Hansard, House of Commons, 1927, Parliamentary Answer by Mr Livingstone, 3 March 1927, Vol 203 cc594–5W.
5 Burridge R and Ormandy D. Eds., *Unhealthy Housing – Research Remedies and Reform* (London: E&FN Spon, 1993).
6 DoE, *Monitoring the New Housing Fitness Standard* (London: DoE, 1993).

7 Legal Research Institute, *Controlling Minimum Standards in Existing Housing* (Warwick University, 1998) main findings available at: www.sabattersby.co.uk/hhsrs/1998_Controlling_Minimum_Standards_Main_Findings.pdf)

8 See, for example, Table A12 in the report *Controlling Minimum Standards in Existing Housing*. Available at: www.sabattersby.co.uk/hhsrs/1998_Controlling_Minimum_Standards_Tables_Annex_of_Tables.pdf

9 Bentley D, *The Future of Private Renting: Shaping a Fairer Market for Tenants and Taxpayers* (London: Civitas: Institute for the Study of Civil Society, 2015). Available at: www.civitas.org.uk/pdf/thefutureofprivaterenting.pdf

10 MHCLG, *English Housing Survey: Private Rented Sector 2016–17* (London: Crown Copyright, 2018).

4   The law of nuisance and statutory nuisance

Introduction

4.01   The law of nuisance is made up of three forms: private nuisance, public nuisance, and statutory nuisance. In this book, we are mainly concerned with statutory nuisance and with its implications for those living in residential property. Private nuisance and public nuisance are creatures of the common law. We need to consider them because they have great significance for the law of statutory nuisance. This is because statutory nuisance is conceptually based on these common law forms of nuisance, and much of the case law is both relevant to and binding on the law of statutory nuisance.

4.02   This case law is also significant because of the way statutory nuisance legislation is drafted in Part III of the Environmental Protection Act 1990. A condition or state of affairs may amount to a statutory nuisance under s.79 of the Act in two ways: either because it is prejudicial to health or a nuisance at common law. This means that, although the type of nuisance must come within the list of statutory nuisances set down in s.79, the scope of the nuisance limb is largely determined by case law.

Private nuisance

4.03   Although there is an overlap between statutory nuisance and private nuisance, this does not mean that they are the same. A private nuisance may be defined as any activity or state of affairs which causes a substantial and unreasonable interference with a neighbour's use or enjoyment of their land. This crossing of a property boundary is fundamentally important. Nuisance cases must involve an activity or condition affecting *neighbouring* property, though this should not be interpreted as being restricted solely to adjoining property. This conception of private nuisance also applies to the nuisance limb of statutory nuisance. In both cases, there is a legal requirement for the problem causing a nuisance to originate on or emanate from one property and to cause harm on neighbouring property.

4.04 The tort of private nuisance is a civil action giving rights to the owners of property to protection from activities carried out on neighbouring property. Besides harmful activities, it may be the condition or state of the property that causes a nuisance to neighbours. A civil action in private nuisance would usually be taken in order to obtain an injunction to prevent it from continuing or recurring. It may also include an application for damages: compensation for loss or damage that resulted from the nuisance.

4.05 Private nuisance covers a wider range of interferences to neighbouring land than statutory nuisance. An encroachment onto a neighbour's land by tree roots, causing damage to the foundations of a block of flats was found to be a private nuisance in *Delaware Mansions*.[1] But this could not be a statutory nuisance because, firstly, this type of problem does not come within the scope of the statutory nuisances listed in s.79 EPA 1990. But there is also a conceptual reason which limits this problem only to a private nuisance action. For a nuisance to come within the scope of statutory nuisance, the harm suffered must interfere with "personal comfort" or be "offensive to the senses" of those occupying or visiting the neighbouring property.[2] If the harm applies only to the property itself or only to household pets, or if the harm only affects the running of a business, then a private nuisance action may offer relief but not a statutory nuisance.

4.06 Rights of ownership in property and land can be protected by the law of private nuisance; hence it is often referred to as a proprietorial tort. Those able to claim such rights include freeholders, leaseholders, and tenants. Private tenants holding assured shorthold tenancies and tenants of a local authority or housing association have rights in property and are able to protect those rights using the law of private nuisance.

4.07 This requirement in private nuisance for a claimant to have a proprietorial interest in land or property does not apply to statutory nuisance. The main purpose of the statutory nuisance regime is to enable local authorities to take enforcement action under s.80 EPA 1990 on behalf of the public and persons affected by statutory nuisances. Thus, a local authority is placed under statutory duties by s.79 EPA 1990 (a) to inspect its area from time to time to detect any statutory nuisances and (b) to respond to a complaint from a person living in its area. A statutory duty is entirely different from a right of action by a claimant in civil proceedings to protect a right or interest.

4.08   Private prosecutions may be brought by "persons aggrieved", under s.82 EPA 1990, in order to resolve statutory nuisances caused by neighbours. This provides a parallel means of enforcement of statutory nuisance law to action taken by the local authority. A "person aggrieved" is a wider category than those having a proprietorial interest, as required in private nuisance proceedings. The term includes anyone who can show that he or she is materially affected by the nuisance and is not restricted to those having proprietorial rights.[3] This type of prosecution can also be employed where the state of a dwelling amounts to a statutory nuisance and the tenant wishes to make their landlord undertake measures to abate it. Section 82 prosecutions can be taken by tenants against their landlords where the landlord is a local authority or a social landlord.

Public nuisance

4.09   Public nuisance comes within the scope of statutory nuisance because the nuisance limb of s.79(1) EPA 1990 includes both public and private nuisances.[4] However, nuisances affecting persons occupying residential property will only rarely amount to a public nuisance, in part because the threshold for liability in public nuisance is a high one. A wide range of circumstances fall within the scope of public nuisance. Examples affecting occupiers of residential property include:

- the emission of noxious smells from a chicken-processing factory;[5]
- allowing refuse and filth to be deposited on vacant land in a densely populated part of London;[6]
- holding noisy events, such as motocross.[7]

4.10   Public nuisance is a long-established common law tort and a crime.[8] It applies to serious behavioural and environmental forms of nuisance in public places which breach the rights of the public. Archbold defines a public nuisance as resulting either from an act not warranted by law or from an omission to discharge a legal duty: "If the effect of the act or omission is to endanger the life, health, property or comfort of the public, or to obstruct the public in the exercise or enjoyment of rights common to all Her Majesty's subjects".[9]

4.11   This is a very wide definition, criticised by some for being vague and much too wide.[10] In order to engage with the nuisance limb of statutory nuisance, a public nuisance will need to endanger "the health and comfort of the public at large".[11] This does not mean that everyone in the neighbourhood must be affected by a public nuisance. But if only a few people are affected or if the nuisance is such that a number of individuals are each separately victims of a private nuisance, then a public nuisance will not be made out. In *R v Rimmington*, Lord Roger opined that "a core element of the issue of public nuisance is that the defendant's act should affect the community, a section of the public, rather than simply individuals".[12]

Statutory nuisance

4.12 In the rest of this chapter, we will be concerned with aspects of the statutory nuisance regime affecting the occupation of residential property. We are particularly concerned with two types of statutory nuisance: first, with those arising from the state of the premises – s.79(1)(a) EPA 1990, and secondly, with noise emitted from premises – s.79(1)(g).

4.13 As with nearly all forms of statutory nuisance, those arising from the state of the premises and noise are required to fall within one or other of the two limbs of the statutory nuisance regime. Section 79 EPA 1990 stipulates that a statutory nuisance must be "prejudicial to health or a nuisance". These two limbs are alternative requirements, but it is not required that an abatement notice drafted to regulate a statutory nuisance stipulates the limb under which the enforcement action is being taken.[13]

4.14 The concept of "prejudicial to health" is purely a creature of statute, developed in the nineteenth century as part of public health law. It originated in the Nuisances Removal and Diseases Prevention Acts of 1848 and 1849. In these early statutes, the wording used was "a nuisance or injurious to health". "Prejudicial to health", which includes injury to health, is defined in s.79(7) of the EPA 1990. It applies in situations where there is a risk to health as well as when actual injury has occurred.

4.15 The nuisance limb, on the other hand, owes its origins to the common law. It must, therefore, satisfy the basic elements of either public or private nuisance.[14] It also requires there to be an interference with "personal comfort" or something that is "offensive to the senses". Whereas the nuisance limb should be interpreted in accordance with the common law, the meaning of the health limb is decided by statute law and any binding decisions of the High Court interpreting the relevant statutes.

4.16 The reasonableness of the offending activity is a basic requirement for establishing the existence of a statutory nuisance falling under the nuisance limb. It will not be relevant, however, when a statutory nuisance has arisen which falls under the health limb. Where there is a threat of illness or disease, no question can arise as to the reasonableness of the action giving rise to the statutory nuisance. This is an important distinction between the two limbs. For example, duration and time of day go to the issue of reasonableness, and this will only be relevant for the nuisance limb. The reasonableness of the offending activity is not in question where prejudice to health is established. So, for example, a sudden and brief escape of fumes (a statutory nuisance under s.79(1)(c) EPA 1990) which causes ill health would not be rendered reasonable because of its short duration.

4.17   The definition of prejudicial to health provided in s.79(7) EPA 1990 is "injurious, or likely to cause injury, to health". The meaning of "likely to cause injury to health" has not been subject to judicial interpretation in relation to statutory nuisance. However, in *Wallis v Bristol Water plc*,[15] the Divisional Court was required to consider the meaning of this phrase in the context of regulations affecting contamination of water. The court took the view that the phrase means that there must be a "real possibility" of injury being caused, given the public health considerations behind the statute. This implies a high standard needing to be met by the person carrying on the activity. They will be liable if it can be shown that there is a "real possibility" of injury rather than the stricter standard of a probability.

State of premises: s.79(1)(a) EPA 1990

4.18   The definition of "premises" given in s.79(7) EPA 1990 includes land and any vessel (unless powered by steam-reciprocating machinery). In *R v Parlby*,[16] it was decided that public sewers are not premises within the meaning of section 79(1)(a). Furthermore, *Parlby* confirms that this provision is confined to cases in which the premises themselves have fallen into such a state and are decayed, dilapidated, dirty, or out of order.

4.19   Most cases in which this type of statutory nuisance occurs fall under the health limb. Where only occupiers are affected by the state of the premises in which they live, it can only fall under the health limb, since there is no element of private or public nuisance present. When this form of statutory nuisance affects neighbouring property then, usually, it would fall under the nuisance limb because it arises on one property but affects another. Even where a property boundary is crossed, it could also fall under the health limb, for health risks which are disease related – such as when the effects of damp arising on one property pose a risk to the health of neighbouring occupiers.

4.20   Section 79(1)(a) EPA 1990 is concerned with the *state* of the premises, not with defects in the layout or faults in design. In *Everett*,[17] the Court of Appeal decided that a steep and dangerous staircase did not come within the scope of the health limb. The court concluded that public health legislators in the nineteenth century were intent on controlling infectious and contagious diseases but were not concerned about the risk of physical injury resulting from the state of premises. The risk of personal injury could not, therefore, come within the scope of this form of statutory nuisance.

4.21   The Court of Appeal in *Everett* could be criticised for taking too narrow an approach in deciding the meaning of "prejudice to health".[18] The majority of their lordships were much influenced by what they thought Parliament intended when the wording of this subsection first received parliamentary scrutiny in 1855.[19] The Court of Appeal was also mindful that the local authority had powers under other legislation to deal with the type of health risk in question. So, in a similar case today, officers should be looking to the Housing Act 2004 and HHSRS for resolution of this kind of problem.[20]

4.22   The restrictiveness of the health limb for statutory nuisances involving the state of premises has been reinforced by later case law. In *Birmingham City Council v Oakley*,[21] the health risks associated with the internal arrangement of the premises was considered. A lavatory lacking a wash-hand basin was located next to the kitchen of the premises, which were owned by Birmingham City Council, acting as the landlord of the Oakley family.[22] In order to wash their hands after using the toilet, members of the family would either have to pass through the kitchen into the bathroom, which led off from the other side of the kitchen, or wash their hands – more conveniently – in the kitchen sink. It was not disputed that this arrangement encouraged an unhygienic practice that could lead to germs being transmitted into an area where food was prepared.

4.23   A majority of the House of Lords in *Oakley* agreed that there was a fundamental distinction to be drawn between the way the premises are used and the state of the premises. In the context of this form of statutory nuisance, it was only the practice resulting from the use of the premises that posed the health risk, not the state of the premises themselves. Furthermore, this was not a case where the existing facilities had fallen into a state of disrepair with the result that those defective facilities formed the risk to health.

4.24   This decision means that problems arising from internal layout and poor design of premises do not come within the scope of the health limb of s.79(1)(a) EPA 1990. *Oakley* is binding for subsequent decisions of the courts, and this decision severely limits the use of the statutory nuisance regime for improving the quality of the housing stock. This is the case even though the source of the risk of disease was attributable to the obsolete layout of the premises and the lack of toilet facilities that one would expect to find nowadays in residential property.

4.25   Another reason for such a conservative stance being taken by the majority in *Oakley* was because the property in question was obsolete and scheduled for demolition. Improvements to the housing stock come within the scope of other legislation; if changes are needed, then the duty of Parliament would be to provide new measures. Lord Millett spoke for the majority in giving a narrow interpretation on the scope of the health limb in s.79(1)(a) EPA 1990:

> *I do not doubt that the presence of a defective drain or lavatory lacking ventilation on the premises is capable of rendering the state of the premises a danger to health. But I do not consider that the complete absence of a lavatory (or a bath or kitchen), however inconvenient, could be said to render the state of the premises injurious to health. There was nothing wrong with the lavatory in the present case except its location. It was not a danger to health. Any danger to health arose from the absence of a washbasin in its vicinity. Whether the law should require washbasins to be installed near lavatories is a matter for Parliament, but the Public Health Acts are not a suitable vehicle. They are concerned with the state of premises and not with their physical layout or the facilities to be provided in them. These are matters for building regulations, which can distinguish between new constructions and old.*[23]

4.26   The application of the health limb to statutory nuisances arising from the state of premises occurs when they have fallen into a "filthy or unwholesome condition".[24] Lord Slynn, in giving the leading speech in *Oakley*, was heavily influenced by the language used by legislators in the 1850s. His lordship continued by describing the scope of the health limb as applying to:

> *the collection of noxious matter or a foul or offensive drain or privy. All of these were in themselves prejudicial to health because of the germs or smells or the risk of disease . . . They*

are directed to the presence in the house of some feature which
is in itself prejudicial to health in that it is a source of possible
infection or disease or illness such as dampness, mould, dirt or
evil smelling accumulations or the presence of rats.

4.27   Many defects in property can be held responsible for risks to health. In *Salford City Council v McNally*,[25] the defects complained of included: an accumulation of refuse, dampness, defective sanitary fittings, unsealed drains allowing egress of rats, defective windows and/ or doors, leaking roof, defective drainage, defective plasterwork, and defective floors. As in *Oakley*, the house was in a slum condition and had been designated for clearance by the local authority. The occupier, as a "person aggrieved" by the statutory nuisance, brought an action against their local authority landlord.[26] The court found, at first instance, that there was rising damp and perished plaster; that the rear door was rotten and unhinged; that there was severe dampness on the first floor; and that the water closet pipe was cracked and insanitary. In view of their serious and extensive nature, these matters were deemed to cause the state of the house to be prejudicial to health. Similarly, in *Patel v Mehtab*,[27] it was held that defects which included dampness, leaks, inadequate ventilation, the presence of fungus, coldness and draughts, and a defective water heater were injurious to health.

4.28   These cases suggest that where tenants (whether of public or private landlords) are exposed to the risk of disease in a property suffering from a series of defects that amount to a serious problem, then s.79(1)(a) EPA 1990 provides an appropriate means to resolve the problem, either by the local authority serving an abatement notice under s.80 of the Act or by the tenant taking action under s.82. But the case law would also suggest that s.79(1)(a) does not provide an appropriate remedy for what is probably the most serious example of a housing defect for many decades: the use of combustible cladding fitted to high-rise flats, such as in Grenfell Tower.[28]

4.29   The limitations in the scope of s.79(1)(a) EPA 1990 resulting from the House of Lords decision in *Oakley* means that inadequate sound insulation in premises cannot be dealt with under this provision. In *Vella*,[29] the Divisional Court held, following *Oakley*, that a lack of adequate sound insulation cannot render premises to be in such a state as to be prejudicial to health under s.79(1)(a). The court agreed that:

if the words used in section 79(1)(a) can be given no wider
meaning than that which has attached to the same words since
the enactment of the 'sanitary statutes' of the mid-nineteenth

> *century, there can be no room for holding that a lack of sound insulation sufficient to comply with current standards renders premises in such a state as to be prejudicial to health.*[30]

4.30 Many s.79(1)(a) cases are concerned with the internal state of residential premises. Typically, these are cases where condensation problems arising from the condition of the dwelling cause dampness, black mould, and other fungal growth within the property. This problem can arise from a lack of proper heating or ventilation or could be caused by structural problems such as the lack of a damp-proof course or cavity walls, or defective plumbing, or from several causes.

4.31 Complaints about dampness are common and need to be investigated carefully in order to establish who bears responsibility. These cases often arise in relation to tenanted properties and may give rise to a clash of viewpoints between landlord and tenant. The former may tend to blame the lifestyle of the latter, while the latter may consider the situation to be the result of neglect or indifference on the part of the landlord. A condensation problem may be caused by the failure of the landlord to provide adequate heating or ventilation facilities. Alternatively, the tenant may not be using the facilities properly and is, therefore, responsible for the statutory nuisance. It is also possible for more than one person to be responsible for a statutory nuisance.[31]

4.32 With tenanted property, if the dampness is caused by a structural problem, the remedy lies in the hands of another person responsible for the structure and exterior of the building. In a chain of leases, for example, the superior landlord might be responsible. The correct person having control must be identified as being responsible for the nuisance so that an appropriate abatement notice may be served.[32]

4.33 In a block of flats, there are likely to be three different types of premises. These are: the building as whole and the common parts – usually under the freeholder's control; the individual flats, in which leaseholders or other types of tenants occupy with rights of exclusive possession. It is important for investigating officers to establish who is responsible for abating the statutory nuisance for the premises in question. So, in a block of flats, the source of the problem may be from the structure of the building or the common parts, the responsibility for abatement lying with the freeholder. Individual leaseholders or tenants may be responsible for statutory nuisances arising on their own property. An evidence-based investigation will be necessary in each case in order to establish who is responsible. In the case of a statutory nuisance arising from any defect of a structural character, an abatement notice should be served on the owner of the premises, under s.80(2)(b) EPA 1990.

4.34 In an appeal against an abatement notice or prosecution for breach of a notice, it may be necessary to provide expert evidence on the health risk to assist the court. The evidence of environmental health officers, housing officers, or surveyors will be accepted as expert evidence, provided that these professionals have relevant experience.[33] The fact that these officers may be employed by the local authority does not prevent them from acting as experts, although the court would need to be satisfied that they were objective in regard to their evidence. Indeed, it is desirable that employed experts are given training on the requirements for giving expert evidence before a court.[34] These include the requirements that such persons have sufficient and relevant expertise in regard to the relevant issues in the case and, secondly, that they are aware that their overriding duty lies with the court and not their employer.

The health limb and other forms of statutory nuisance

4.35 The limited scope of the health limb to the risk of disease or illness applies not only to the state of premises but to other forms of public health statutory nuisance originating in the mid-nineteenth century. The list of public health nuisances from s.79(1) EPA 1990 comprises: the state of any premises; emissions of smoke from premises; any dust, steam, smell or other effluvia arising on industrial, trade, or business premises; any accumulation or deposit; the keeping of animals.[35] Statutory nuisances coming under the Public Health Act 1936 should also be included in this list.[36]

4.36 The health effects of more recent forms of statutory nuisance, such as those resulting from fumes and gases emitted from domestic premises, are limited to illnesses directly linked to ingestion. For insects emanating from relevant industrial, trade, or business premises, there would have to be a link to illness or disease caused by exposure to the insects in question. Amenity forms of statutory nuisance – those arising from noise or artificial light – involve a different type of health risk from that encompassed by the older public health nuisances There is no decided case law on whether consequential mental illnesses could come within the scope of the health limb for these recent forms of statutory nuisance, but the point is arguable.

Noise emitted from premises: s.79(1)(g) EPA 1990

4.37 By contrast with statutory nuisances resulting from the state of premises, noise nuisances usually engage the nuisance limb of s.79(1) EPA 1990. The threshold for noise nuisance is a high one: statutory nuisance action has never been intended to regulate mere annoyances or to protect amenity to the same extent as can be required with conditions attached to the grant of planning permission. Noise problems falling below the threshold for nuisance may, however, come within the scope of provisions in the Anti-social Behaviour, Crime and Policing Act 2014.[37]

4.38   Whereas to the lay person anything annoying may be perceived as a nuisance, the legal test for noise nuisance – whether based on measurements or not – is objective: the noise must be both excessive and unreasonable. Probably more than for any other form of statutory nuisance, with noise there are wide variations between the perceptions of individuals and their ability to tolerate it. Much depends on the personality of the persons affected, on their lifestyle and cultural background, and on other aspects of their life.

4.39   Persons affected by noise from their neighbours may become oversensitised, particularly where the neighbour causing the noise does not respond to complaints. Developing oversensitivity because of long-term exposure to noise is understandable and should not mean that a complainant's account will not be accepted. But the threshold for noise nuisance is high, the standard is objective, and individuals may have to put up with a certain level of annoyance. In *Walter v Selfe*, this issue was posed colourfully:

> *[O]ught this inconvenience to be considered as more than fanciful, more than one of mere delicacy or fastidiousness, as an inconvenience materially interfering with the ordinary comfort physically of human existence, not merely according to elegant or dainty modes of living, but according to plain and sober and simple notions among the English people?*[38]

Establishing liability for statutory noise nuisance

4.40   Reaching a decision that a complaint amounts to a statutory nuisance requires that all the relevant factors be weighed up and assessed properly. Frequently, issues are not clear-cut, so care and professionalism are needed if decisions are to be made both properly and fairly. Investigating officers should take an independent and objective view of the situation and not be over-influenced by the persuasiveness of complainants.[39] Relevant factors to consider include:

- the level and type of noise;
- duration and how often the noise occurs;

- the time of day or night when the noise occurs;
- whether any aggravating characteristics are present;
- what measures could reduce or modify the noise;
- the characteristics of the neighbourhood where the noise occurs;
- the number of persons affected; and
- whether best practicable means (BPM) have been used to control noise emanating from industrial, trade, or business premises.

4.41 The approach adopted by the local authority to control noise problems should include advice and persuasion rather than proceeding headlong down a road leading to prosecution. Balancing this, however, is a statutory duty to serve an abatement notice under s.80 of the EPA 1990 once the point has been reached that the local authority is satisfied that a nuisance exists or is likely to occur or recur. Subsections (2A) to (2E) of s.80 allow a period of up to seven days for the local authority, if it chooses, to delay serving a noise abatement notice if it believes that some other action may resolve the noise nuisance.[40]

4.42 The standard of proof required to serve an abatement notice is the civil standard: on the balance of probabilities. In cases investigated by local authorities under s.80 EPA 1990, it is the opinion of the local authority, as set down in the abatement notice which defines the boundary of the nuisance. Crucial in establishing the reasonableness of that opinion is the quality of the evidence employed to justify service of the abatement notice. Evidence that will assist the court includes: complainants' noise diaries, reported effects, subjective observations, and noise monitoring. A contemporaneous note made by officers of the extent and type of noise will also be relevant. There is no legal requirement for investigating officers to take noise measurements before making a decision about noise nuisance. However, in the light of the decision in *Rottenberg*,[41] as a matter of good practice, clear reasons should be given for deciding not to obtain scientific noise readings.

Neighbour or domestic noise

4.43 Domestic noise comprises a large and growing body of complaints to local authorities.[42] Incidents may occur because of thoughtless or selfish, rather than deliberate behaviour. Complaints can be triggered by a range of activities, including the playing of amplified music and musical instruments, holding noisy parties, performing DIY and car repairs, and barking dogs.

4.44 Particular problems arise in residential areas with high population densities, particularly where the standard of noise insulation between properties is inadequate. Poor sound insulation may make noise problems intolerable or mean that the everyday sounds of ordinary living cause considerable annoyance and nuisance to neighbours. This will often be the case with older flats and house conversions in both the private and social housing sectors. Close proximity of residents having different social class, cultural, or ethnic backgrounds may exacerbate the problem.

4.45 The volume, quality of sound, the times, frequency, and duration of the noise are all highly relevant to the question of establishing statutory nuisance. Domestic noise nuisance – as with all forms of nuisance – is subject to the test of "reasonable user" or the principle of give and take. This requires the person causing the alleged nuisance to consider not only whether his or her own use of the property is reasonable but the effect this use has on the neighbour. The point was well made by Lord Millett in *Baxter v Camden LBC*:

> It is not enough for a landowner to act reasonably in his own interest. He must also be considerate of the interest of his neighbour. The governing principle is good neighbourliness, and this involves reciprocity. A landowner must show the same consideration for his neighbour as he would expect his neighbour to show for him.[43]

4.46 Does this mean that a statutory nuisance is established if the everyday noise of a resident interferes with his neighbour's use and enjoyment of property? Poor sound insulation between adjoining properties often triggers complaints. Standards of sound insulation set down in the Building Regulations are arguably inadequate, relying on building materials having "reasonable resistance" to the transmission of airborne or impact sound.[44] With such a low standard, the potential for noise complaints is high, especially where properties are converted into flats. Unless there is an unreasonable element, normal everyday noise will not constitute a private nuisance, and therefore there will be no statutory nuisance. In other words, it is not reasonable to expect neighbours to behave especially quietly because the sound insulation between their properties is poor. Lord Hoffmann in *Baxter v Camden LBC* argued that:

> I do not think that the normal use of a residential flat can possibly be a nuisance to the neighbours. If it were, we would have

the absurd position that each, behaving normally and reasonably, was a nuisance to the other.[45]

In such cases, a more appropriate and sustainable solution can be obtained if the parties involved are prepared to use community mediation to resolve their dispute.

4.47 The key variable is "normal use", so a nuisance would require some additional, unreasonable aspect. This might include, for example, placing domestic appliances against an adjoining wall unnecessarily, using such equipment during sleeping hours, or playing musical instruments over long periods. The concept of normal use does not address the issue that what is normal and everyday for one person may not be for another because of differing lifestyles.

One-off events

4.48 Complaints are frequently made about one-off events, such as noisy parties, especially when these are held late at night. Some local authorities, especially in urban areas, employ "party patrols" in order to deal with such complaints. Unless there is a pattern of complaints, local authorities will generally balk at using statutory nuisance powers. The nuisance limb of statutory nuisance requires there to be "an interference for a substantial period with the use and enjoyment of neighbouring property".[46] This suggests that the noise problem would need to have an element of continuity to reach the threshold for nuisance. In a very serious case involving a one-off event, this might amount to a public nuisance, where the continuity element derived from private nuisance does not apply. A public nuisance would be actionable under the nuisance limb of statutory nuisance.[47]

4.49 Powers available under the Noise Act 1996 are often a more appropriate and proportionate way to control one-off noise events, though these powers are only available to control night-time noise, between 11 p.m. and 7 a.m. However, few local authorities (Belfast City Council being a notable exception) utilise the powers available to them under this legislation.

The defence of best practicable means

4.50 The fact that a locality is a noisy one or of an industrial character does not in itself constitute a defence to nuisance. The reasonability issue central to nuisance focuses not just on the activity itself but also on the effects that the activity has on neighbouring users. In *Rushmer v Polsue and Alfieri Ltd*, Cozens-Hardy LJ opined:

> *It does not follow that because I live, say in the manufacturing part of Sheffield I cannot complain if a steam-hammer is introduced next door, and so worked as to render sleep at night almost impossible, although previously to its introduction my house was a reasonably comfortable abode, having regard to the local standard; and it would be no answer to say that the steam-hammer is of the most approved pattern and is reasonably worked.*[48]

4.51   When deciding whether a noise problem amounts to a statutory nuisance, the local authority will need to consider, as part of that decision, whether reasonable steps have been taken to mitigate it. For noise emitted from industrial, trade, and business premises, the local authority should also consider whether best practicable means (BPM) have been used.[49] This statutory defence will be relevant to commercial and industrial noise and to noise emitted from pubs and clubs, since these are trade premises.

4.52   Best practicable means is a statutory defence, and it is for the court to decide whether it has been made out. It can be raised at two stages: when appealing against the service of an abatement notice or as a defence in a prosecution brought for breach of the notice. In either case, it will be up to the noise producer to prove, to a civil standard, that BPM have been used to prevent or to counteract the effects of the nuisance. Practitioners should note that the BPM requirements under the Act include "counteracting the effects" of the noise, so full abatement is not the test.

4.53   It is good practice for the local authority to decide whether BPM have been employed before service of an abatement notice. The basis for doing so is that a noise producer may be able to show that by employing BPM, the use of the land is reasonable and does not amount to a nuisance. Deciding whether BPM have been employed may require expert advice, which may go beyond the expertise of environmental health practitioners (EHPs). If this is the case, the authority will need to decide whether to accept the opinion of the noise producer's expert or to instruct its own expert. Expert advice may be needed to help to decide whether a nuisance has been caused and, if so, to determine the form of notice the authority should serve on the noise producer.

4.54   Consideration of BPM by the local authority at this early stage is relevant to the reasonableness of the decision as to whether a statutory nuisance exists. This is an issue of good practice. But EHPs should note that one of the grounds for appealing a notice is that BPM have been used to counteract the effects of the nuisance.[50] Local authorities need to avoid interpreting their duty under s.80 of the EPA 1990 as a way of obliging businesses to adopt too high a standard of abatement. They have no powers to require the most expensive, best available, or state-of-the-art technology to reduce noise problems to a minimum.

Notes

1 *Delaware Mansions Ltd and Flecksun Ltd v Westminster City Council* [2001] UKHL 55.
2 *Salford City Council v McNally* [1976] AC 379, 389.
3 The EPA 1990 does not give a definition of a "person aggrieved". Lord Esher MR opined in *Re Reed, Bowen & Co, ex p Official Receiver* [1887] 19 QBD 178: "The words 'person aggrieved' are of wide import and should not be subjected to a restrictive interpretation. They do not include, of course, a mere busybody who is interfering in things which do not concern him; but they do include a person who has a genuine grievance . . . which prejudicially affects his interests".
4 *National Coal Board v Neath BC (or Thorne)* [1976] 2 All ER 478.
5 *Shoreham by Sea Urban DC v Dolphin Canadian Proteins* 71 [1972] LGR 26.
6 *Attorney General v Tod Heatley* [1897] 1 ch 560.
7 *East Dorset DC v Eaglebeam Ltd* [2006] EWHC 2378 (QB).
8 In Scotland, there is no distinction between public and private nuisances; nuisances affecting public places are usually dealt with under negligence principles. Public nuisance is not a criminal offence under Scots law.
9 Archbold JF, *Criminal Pleading, Evidence and Practice* (London: Sweet & Maxwell, 2018), para 31–40.
10 Spencer JR, *Public Nuisance: A Critical Examination* [1989] 48 CLJ, 55.
11 *Colour Quest Ltd and ors v Total Downstream UK plc and ors (Rev1)* [2009] EWHC 540 (Comm), para 434.
12 *R v Rimmington* [2005] UKHL 63, para 47.
13 *Lowe and Watson v South Somerset DC* [1998] Env LR 242.
14 *National Coal Board v Neath BC (or Thorne)* [1976] 2 All ER 478.
15 [2009] EWIIC 3432 (Admin).
16 [1889] 22 QBD 520. This decision was based on a similarly worded section of the Public Health Act 1875.
17 *R v Bristol City Council, ex p Everett* [1999] 1 WLR 1170.
18 For a critique of the decisions in *Everett* and *Oakley*, see Malcolm R and Pointing J, Statutory Nuisance: The Sanitary Paradigm and Judicial Conservatism, *Journal of Environmental Law* Vol. 18, No. 1 (2006), 37–54.
19 Nuisances Removal and Diseases Prevention Act 1855.
20 See Chapter 5.
21 *Birmingham City Council v Oakley* [2001] 1 All ER 385.
22 A tenant may bring a statutory nuisance prosecution against their landlord, including where the landlord is a local authority, as a "person aggrieved" under s.82 EPA 1990.
23 *Birmingham City Council v Oakley* [2001] 1 All ER 385, 401–402.

46   *The law of nuisance and statutory nuisance*

24 *Ibid.*, 392.
25 [1976] AC 379.
26 The action was brought by the occupier against the landlord under the Public Health Act 1936, for what would now be a prosecution under s.82 EPA 1990.
27 [1980] 5 HLR 78.
28 See ch 7.17–7.19.
29 *R (on the application of Vella) v Lambeth* LBC [2005] EWHC 2473 (Admin).
30 *Ibid.*, 69.
31 Section 81(1) EPA 1990.
32 The local authority has the power to make requisitions on the land: Local Government (Miscellaneous Provisions) Act 1976, s.16.
33 *Southwark LBC v Simpson* [1999] Env LR 553.
34 *Field v Leeds City Council* [2000] EG 165.
35 See Table 2.1, ch 2.08.
36 See ch 2.36.
37 See ch 7.20–7.28.
38 [1851] 4 DeG & Sm 315, 322.
39 Useful guidance for carrying out investigations can be found in: *Neighbourhood Noise Policies and Practice for Local Authorities – A Management Guide* (CIEH/ Defra, 2006).
40 Such other action could include serving a community protection notice under the Anti-social Behaviour, Crime and Policing Act 2014 or using the provisions of the Noise Act 1996.
41 *R (on the application of Hackney LBC) v Rottenberg* [2007] EWHC 166 (Admin).
42 According to CIEH statistics over 70% of all noise complaints concern domestic noise.
43 *Southwark LBC v Tanner and others; Baxter v Camden LBC (No 2)* [2001] 1 AC 1, 20.
44 Building Regulations, SI 2000/2531, sch 1, Part E.
45 *Southwark LBC v Tanner and others; Baxter v Camden LBC (No 2)* [2001] 1 AC 1, 15.
46 *National Coal Board v Neath BC (or Thorne)* [1976] 2 All ER 478.
47 A public nuisance action for an injunction or prosecution could be undertaken by a local authority using its powers under s.222 of the Local Government Act 1972.
48 [1906] 1 ch 234, 250.
49 EPA 1990, ss.80(7)(8).
50 Statutory Nuisance (Appeals) Regulations 1995, SI 1995/2644, reg. 2(2)(e).

5 HHSRS and Part 1 Housing Act 2004

Procedural and practice issues

Duty to keep conditions under review and direction

5.01 Local housing authorities (LHAs) are required to keep conditions in the housing stock under review and identify any action necessary, including under Parts 1, 2, 3, and 4 of the Housing Act 2004 and the Regulatory Reform (Housing Assistance) England and Wales Order 2002,[1] which is to do with financial assistance for housing renewal.

5.02 By virtue of s.3 of the Act, LHAs must:

- comply with any directions from the appropriate national authority (none yet given); and
- keep records as required by the appropriate national authority.

The only direction issued thus far was in May 2018 as a result of the Grenfell Tower tragedy.[2] In this, the Secretary of State directed that all LHAs, "pursuant to powers under s.3(3) of the Act in carrying out their duty to review housing conditions in their area", have to:

a *take particular regard, when reviewing housing conditions in their area, to the Department's consolidated advice[3] and MHCLG's Independent Expert Advisory Panel's view that Aluminium Composite Material (ACM) with an unmodified polyethylene filler (category 3 in screening tests) with any type of insulation presents a significant fire hazard on buildings over 18m;*

b *take all appropriate steps to identify and notify the MHCLG of all high-rise residential buildings over 18m in their area with a view to identifying any action they should take in accordance with their duties under the Act, including carrying out inspections and assessments of hazards; and*

c *carry out a review to consider any fire safety hazards arising out of potentially unsafe ACM cladding on high-rise residential buildings in their area.*

5.03   The Secretary of State also reminded LHAs that under the Housing Act 2004, local housing authorities and their officers must:

a   *comply with any directions (s.3(3)(a));*

b   *keep such records (and supply them) as the Secretary of State may specify (s.3(3)(b));*

c   *have due regard to any guidance issued by the Secretary of State of Housing, Communities and Local Government about exercising their functions under the Housing Act 2004 (section 9(2)); and*

d   *to take all necessary enforcement action where appropriate.*

Inspections and complaints

5.04   Authorities are also required to undertake an inspection of a property if they consider that this is appropriate to establish whether Category 1 or Category 2 hazards exist. Section 4(2) of the 2004 Act requires that, if there is an official complaint about the condition of a residential premises (that is a complaint made by a JP, Parish or Community Council), the proper officer of the LHA must inspect (and this must entail inspecting the whole of the dwelling), and, where a Category 1 or Category 2 hazard exists, submit a written report without delay to the authority which sets out his or her opinion. The action taken by LHAs will depend upon the existence of Category 1 and Category 2 hazards in houses, which will be determined by a prescribed method – the Housing Health and Safety Rating System (HHSRS). In the case of Category 1 hazards, it will be mandatory to take one of the courses of action set down in the Act (s.5).

5.05   While it is not known whether there are many "official complaints", local authorities should not rely solely on complaints from tenants. Reliance on such complaints would be unlikely to ensure that the worst premises are identified. It would also mean that irresponsible landlords are difficult to identify as their tenants are probably the least likely individuals to complain, being vulnerable in many ways, including retaliatory eviction by the landlord (considered further later in the chapter).

5.06   Local authorities should also take into account any complaints and concerns from other bodies, such as General Practitioner surgeries, Citizens Advice, and other advice agencies operating in the area. It is arguable that enforcement policies should be developed in conjunction with such "partner" organisations, who should be aware of how issues on housing conditions will be handled in order for them to provide sound advice. Housing interventions can keep people out of hospital and also allow timely discharge from hospital, so nurturing links with the NHS can be important too.

Power of entry

5.07 An inspection should only be carried out by a person properly authorised, in writing, by the LHA to determine whether any functions under Part 1 (or Parts 2–4) of the Housing Act 2004 should be exercised. Notice of at least twenty-four hours should be given to the owner (if known) and the occupier of the property. It does not matter whether the inspection is triggered by a complaint or otherwise (for example, as part of an initiative to deal with poor-quality housing). It is not necessary to go to inordinate lengths to identify the owner, but reasonable enquiries should be made. Notice should be given in writing, although if the landlord has previously agreed to electronic communication, then this could be by email, as allowed for under the Civil Procedure Rules. Where contact is initially made by telephone, it must be followed up by written notice. It is worth noting any comments made on the telephone, as these can be taken into account at a later time should it be necessary to decide on the most appropriate course of action.

5.08 Failure to give written notice can invalidate any future action, as it can give grounds for a successful appeal.[4] So long as reasonable efforts have been made to comply with technical requirements, then, from the reported decisions, the Tribunal is unlikely to find the action invalid.[5]

5.09 Notice is not required, however, where the purpose of the inspection is to determine whether there has been an offence under the licensing provisions (failure to obtain a licence). Furthermore, notice is not required for inspecting for over-occupation of a licensed HMO, or for other breaches of licence conditions, or a breach of selective licensing requirements, or breach of the HMO Management Regulations.[6] Even when notice is not required, the inspection must still be carried out at a "reasonable time".

5.10 Guidance published by LACORS (Local Government Regulation) includes the opinion that it is not necessary to give twenty-four hours' notice to the owner and occupier if the LHA has been contacted by the occupier and invited to carry out an inspection.[7] It is argued in the guidance that the authorised officer is not formally exercising his or her power of entry but simply responding to a request from the occupier. However, should conditions be found in the property which result in action having to be taken, this could lead to complications and delay while notice is given for a formal inspection.

5.11   In one case, the local authority (Trafford MDC) had entered the premises with the Fire and Rescue Service (F&RS), and thus the provisions of the Fire and Rescue Services Act 2004 became an additional consideration.[8] At issue was the local authority officer's right to enter the premises for the purpose of issuing an Emergency Prohibition Order. The applicant maintained that she had not given permission for the officers from the LHA to enter the property. She argued that the LHA had failed to comply with s.239(6) of the Housing Act 2004. Trafford contended that they had entered under the provisions of ss.44–46 of the Fire and Rescue Services Act 2004 with officers from the F&RS. The Tribunal concluded, having considered the provisions under which the F&RS had entered the property, that the LHA did not have a right of entry to undertake an inspection in these circumstances, and therefore the Emergency Prohibition Order was invalid and the appeal succeeded. The Tribunal took the view that s.40 of the Housing Act 2004 enables a local authority to enter the premises at any time in order to take emergency remedial action. However, s.40(3) limits emergency remedial action to premises in which action could be taken by issuing an Improvement Notice, under s.11 of the Act. The Tribunal decided that s.40(6) of the Act applied only to emergency remedial action and did not apply to an inspection required to issue an Emergency Prohibition Order. Notice would be required, therefore, as there was no right of entry.

"Better regulation" and the regulators' code

5.12   The relatively low level of use of the powers set down in the 2004 Housing Act can partly be attributed to the government's policy on "better regulation". This policy has been promoted for several years through the issuing, at frequent intervals, of statutory guidance and codes by the Better Regulation Delivery Office and its predecessor bodies. The Regulators' Code now in force was published in April 2014.[9]

5.13   The Code is commonly misunderstood by officers and local housing authorities, who believe that they are obliged to use "informal" routes to secure compliance before using their powers under the Housing Act 2004. The provisions of the 2004 Act accord with better regulation principles if the legislation is followed correctly. The Act provides a range of tools to address problems, so that the method of enforcement can be proportionate to the risks posed to occupiers and also reflect the attitude of the landlord or person responsible for the conditions of the residential accommodation.

5.14 Regulators must have regard to the principles set down in s.21 of the Legislative and Regulatory Reform Act 2006, namely:

a *regulatory activities should be carried out in a way which is transparent, accountable, proportionate and consistent;*

b *regulatory activities should be targeted only at cases in which action is needed.*

The Regulators' Code specifies that the approach taken by regulators should be proportionate but not based on informal methods.

Regulators should avoid imposing unnecessary regulatory burdens through their regulatory activities and should assess whether similar social, environmental and economic outcomes could be achieved by less burdensome means. Regulators should choose proportionate approaches to those they regulate, based on relevant factors including, for example, business size and capacity.[10]

5.15 The LHA should have a clear approach to using the provisions in the Housing Act 2004, which includes a policy setting out how their strategy for dealing with poor housing conditions will be implemented. This should include their approach to identifying and dealing with the landlords of properties in poor condition and indeed how they will deal with "criminal" or "rogue" landlords. They should provide clear information on what the responsibilities of landlords are and what can be done to assist with compliance. In this regard, use can be made of the guidance on the HHSRS for landlords and property-related professionals.

5.16 It is also expected that LHAs as regulators will have a clear complaints procedure. This is not so much for complaints about housing conditions, but there needs to be a system in place to enable people affected by the quality of the service to make representations. In the main, this has focussed on those "regulated", that is the landlords, yet there is no reason why it should not be extended to those living in properties that pose a risk to their health and safety, and where the LHA has not used its powers or has failed to meet its statutory duty.

5.17 The "better regulation" approach assumes that enforcement action is proportionate to the risks involved. That is implicit in Part 1 of the Housing Act 2004 in two ways. First, the HHSRS assesses the severity of risks arising in the property but does not dictate the course of action. Secondly, a range of actions are available in Part 1 that can be used to reflect not only the risks but also a variety of other factors, including the attitude and record of the landlord. If the correct Housing Act procedures are followed, then it follows that the Code will be complied with, and the temptation to act "informally" should not apply. See also Hull Landlords Association v Hull City Council [2019] EWHC 332 (Admin).

5.18   LHAs can ensure consistent enforcement practice by providing regular training. First, there needs to be consistent quality of inspection to ensure that the process of deciding on the most appropriate course of action is properly made. Secondly, the same factors should always be considered during inspections. The notion of consistency does not mean that the same course of action is always taken. It is not unreasonable to take a different course of action where the landlord has failed to comply with notices, or has been convicted of related offences, or has used retaliatory eviction. It would be proportionate to take a more burdensome approach with such a landlord compared to another who has always carried out works that have been required and complied with notices. The statement of reasons required under the Housing Act, s.8 should ensure that the reasons for taking any action are explicit and clear.

5.19   Parts 1–4 of the Housing Act 2004 became a specified enactment as a result of an amendment to Schedule 3 of the Regulatory Enforcement and Sanctions Act 2008.[11] This means that the Primary Authority provisions apply to Part 1 of the 2004 Act and the HHSRS. This is relevant where a landlord has properties in more than one local housing authority area. Primary Authority arrangements can include coordinated partnerships where a group of businesses share an approach to compliance and where the coordination role is usually undertaken by a third party. As at March 2019 there were no Primary Authority partnerships for the Housing Act 2004.

Retaliatory eviction and the Deregulation Act 2015

5.20   An Assured Shorthold Tenancy (AST), operating under s.19A or s.20 of the Housing Act 1988, is protected from retaliatory eviction by s.33 of the Deregulation Act 2015. Landlords are required to provide all new tenants with information about their rights and responsibilities as tenants. Landlords cannot serve a Housing Act 1988, s.21 notice to regain possession of the property unless they have complied with certain legal requirements at the start of the tenancy. A new standard form must be used by the landlord when evicting a tenant under the "no fault", s.21 procedure.

5.21   Where the local authority has served an Improvement Notice or Notice of Emergency remedial action under the Housing Act 2004, tenants are protected from eviction for six months from the date of service of the notice, regardless of whether they have previously raised the issue with the landlord. Where a tenant has been served with an s.21 notice and is seeking to have it found invalid, he or she will need to have raised the complaint with the landlord beforehand.

5.22   The Department for Communities and Local Government (DCLG, now MHCLG, Ministry of Housing, Communities and Local Government) guidance on retaliatory eviction under the Deregulation Act 2015 says: "[T]enants should always report any disrepair or poor conditions that may arise to the landlord as soon as possible. They should put their complaint in writing".[12] The landlord must respond within fourteen days to the tenant making a complaint. If the landlord responds by issuing an s.21 eviction notice, the tenant should approach his or her local authority and ask them to step in and carry out an inspection to verify the need for the repair. This will not be needed where the local authority has carried out an inspection on its own initiative.

5.23   This protection does not apply where the fault lies with the tenant for the condition of the dwelling-house or common parts that gave rise to service of the notice.[13] The tenant is under an implied duty to use the dwelling-house in a tenant-like manner, and there may be an express term in the tenancy agreement to that effect. The provisions do not apply when at the time the s.21 notice is issued, the dwelling-house is genuinely on the market for sale.[14]

5.24   Local authorities should consider whether they are providing sufficient advice and support to tenants to enable them to complain in writing and are fully aware of the provisions in this legislation. In particular, it is essential for tenants to be aware that they must approach the landlord in the first instance to carry out repairs. The protection from retaliatory eviction depends on the landlord responding unlawfully to the tenant's complaint about repairs.

5.25   Local housing authorities need to make these provisions known to tenants and to publicise them via advice agencies. Publicity for this provision should form part of an authority's approach to regulating the private rented sector. The protection from eviction afforded to tenants by the Deregulation Act 2015 is limited. It does not apply at all if the action taken by the local housing authority is under the statutory nuisance provisions of the EPA 1990. This is an important consideration when it comes to deciding which provision to use – the

Housing Act 2004 or the Environmental Protection Act 1990 – to resolve a problem of housing conditions.

5.26   If the deficiencies identified in an inspection contribute to hazards that pose a risk to safety, then there is no choice as to whether to use the Housing Act 2004 (Part 1) or the statutory nuisance provisions in the Environmental Protection Act 1990. The risk of physical injury is excluded from the health limb of statutory nuisance.[15]

Quality of inspection

5.27   The inspection to identify deficiencies is the first and crucial part of the process of using the HHSRS. The inspection and hazard assessment must be carried out in accordance with the appropriate regulations; in England, these are the Housing Health and Safety Rating System (England) Regulations 2005.[16] The HHSRS is based on a whole dwelling inspection. This is required because a number of defects or deficiencies can contribute to a single hazard. So, for example, even if there is dampness of different forms in different parts of the dwelling, the hazard of Damp and Mould is rated only once. In the same way, the steps and stairs throughout the whole letting, including in the gardens and access to the property, have to be examined to identify any deficiencies; wherever located, they will all contribute to the hazard of Falling on Stairs etc. The common parts should also be included where the dwelling is in a multi-occupied building.

5.28   The Regulations require that an inspector must have regard to any guidance given under s.9 of the Housing Act 2004 in relation to the inspection of residential premises – that is the Operating Guidance. The inspector must also inspect any residential premises with a view to preparing an accurate record of their state and condition and prepare and keep such a record in written or electronic form. This means that the inspector should keep a record of the inspection and findings and should rate the hazards identified at the time of the inspection. It seems that often hazards ratings are not done until such time as "negotiations" with landlords fail and/or after it is decided that a particular course of action will be taken. This is the wrong way around. If action is to be proportional to the risks, then the hazard rating should be prepared before any further action is taken.

5.29   An example of how this can go awry – also reflecting on the poor competence of the inspector – was shown in an appeal concerning Hambleton DC in the then Residential Property Tribunal.[17] Here, housing association tenants in a semi-detached house complained that there was a noise problem from the adjoining property that had been converted into two flats with local authority Building Regulation approval. The EHO investigating the case first thought it was appropriate to use the Noise and Statutory Nuisance Act 1993 and asked the complainant to keep a diary. It was decided subsequently that the 1993 Act provided no remedy in this situation. However, it was also decided by the local authority that the noise was considered to be Category 1 HHSRS hazard, and an Improvement Notice was served on the housing association landlord of the complainant. The appeal by the housing association was on the ground that, as part of the problem was due to the lack of a party wall in the roof space, the owner of the adjoining property should contribute to the cost of works.

5.30 Although upholding the appeal, the Tribunal did decide that the noise was a Category 1 hazard. The local authority was criticised for the way the inspection had been carried out. Its evidence included an inaccurate description of the property, including giving an incorrect number of bedrooms. Nor had there been any reference made to the other hazards, such as fire, that arose from the deficiencies found in the inspection. The Tribunal decided that, even if the problem was due entirely to the lack of a complete party wall in the roof space, the remedial action was excessive. However, the local authority's case was not lost because of its poor case management. The appeal was decided on a point of law. The neighbouring owner had no legal interest in the property that was the subject of the notice, so therefore could not be required to contribute to the cost.

HHSRS hazards

5.31 There are twenty-nine HHSRS hazards (see table 5.1). A hazard in this context is any risk of harm to the health or safety of an actual or potential occupier that arises from a deficiency or deficiencies. So, after the inspection has identified the deficiencies, the inspector has to be able to think in terms of the "effect of the defect" and specify what hazard is involved. In some cases, as well as being a hazard in its own right, a hazard may increase the likelihood of an occurrence or severity of harm linked to another hazard. Harm in this context is an "adverse physical or mental effect on the health of a person". It includes physical injury, as well as an illness, condition or symptom – whether physical or mental. It also includes both permanent and temporary harm. For the purposes of the HHSRS, the possible harms that may result from an occurrence are categorised according to their perceived severity into four classes. In all cases, these are harms of sufficient severity to be fatal or require medical attention and therefore be recorded in hospital admissions or general practitioner (GP) records.

Table 5.1 The 29 HHSRS hazards

A Physiological requirements

Hygrothermal conditions

 1 Damp and mould growth
 2 Excess cold
 3 Excess heat

Pollutants (non-microbial)

 4 Asbestos (and MMF)
 5 Biocides
 6 Carbon monoxide and fuel combustion products
 7 Lead
 8 Radiation
 9 Uncombusted fuel gas
10 Volatile organic compounds

B Psychological requirements

Space, security, light, and noise

11 Crowding and space
12 Entry by intruders
13 Lighting
14 Noise

C Protection against infection

Hygiene, sanitation, and water supply

15 Domestic hygiene, pests, and refuse
16 Food safety
17 Personal hygiene, sanitation, and drainage
18 Water supply

D Protection against accidents

19 Falls associated with baths, etc.
20 Falling on level surfaces, etc.
21 Falling on stairs, etc.
22 Falling between levels

Electric shocks, fires, burns, and scalds

23 Electrical hazards
24 Fire
25 Flames, hot surfaces, etc.

Collisions, cuts, and strains

26 Collision and entrapment
27 Explosions
28 Position and operability of amenities, etc.
29 Structural collapse and failing elements

5.32 It is not our intention in this monograph to set out how the HHSRS works in detail but to provide some important pointers and discuss matters that should be borne in mind by practitioners. The main focus of the work is on procedures after the hazard has been rated.

5.33 Identifying the deficiency and relating it to a hazard may be the only way to resolve a problem. Where noise disturbance is not attributable to noise being emitted from premises but to a lack of sound attenuation between dwellings, the Housing Act 2004 may be the only route for securing a remedy. In *Vella*,[18] the lack of adequate sound insulation did not cause the premises to be in such a state as to come within the prejudicial to health limb of s.79(1) EPA 1990. This limitation does not apply to Part 1 of the Housing Act 2004, as hazards can arise from deficiencies attributable to poor design and low standards of build as well as disrepair.

5.34 The general procedure for using the HHSRS can be summarised as:

1 Inspect and identify deficiencies (which can be the result of design, disrepair, materials used, form of construction, deterioration, disrepair, or a lack of maintenance).

2 Identify the hazards arising from the deficiencies.

3 Rate the hazards identified, where the likelihood of an occurrence over the next twelve months is considered to be greater than average, as set out in the Operating Guidance, considering the actual likelihood and spread of harms using the methodology as set out in the Regulations[19] (failure to do so could render the assessment invalid). This assessment is made by reference to any vulnerable age group that has been identified in the guidance. The actual current occupiers should be ignored. This means an empty property can be assessed and that this should be an objective assessment.

5.35 This is set out in more detail along with the hazard profiles for all twenty-nine hazards in the statutory Operating Guidance,[20] to which all officers using the HHSRS should have regard. The appropriate Tribunal, when dealing with appeals or other cases under Part 1 of the 2004 Act, should also have regard to the Operating Guidance. It was apparent from responses to the CIEH Survey and Report – "HHSRS 11 Years on"[21] – that a number of respondents criticised the system because certain matters, so it was said, could not be dealt with under the HHSRS. However, it was apparent they had not read the Operating Guidance carefully as these matters are covered. Also, there might have been some confusion in the minds of some respondents between the HHSRS – a system for assessing and communicating the seriousness of risk – and Part 1 of the 2004 Act. Anyone using the HHSRS should always check the Operating Guidance, which lists those matters that may contribute to the chance of an occurrence happening with possible harmful outcomes. However, this is only the starting point, and officers can use any appropriate evidence to support their judgements when assessing the hazard.[22]

Part 1 Housing Act 2004

5.36   Reference has already been made to the duties under the Housing Act 2004. The Act itself does not mention the HHSRS, but only Category 1 and Category 2 hazards. Category 1 hazards are those that have a hazard score of 1000 or more – using the HHSRS – and Category 2 hazards are those scoring 999 or less. Local authorities are under a duty to take one of the courses of action set out in the Act. For Category 2 hazards, they have a discretion to act. In a way, this makes the decision more difficult as it will be necessary to show why and how that discretion has been used. It should be noted that Category 2 hazards could still pose a significant risk to the health of occupiers. For Category 1 hazards, the only decision is over which provision is the most appropriate to use.

5.37   The powers available to address hazards (where no management order is in force) under Part 1 of the 2004 Act are to serve:

- *Improvement Notices*[23] (which may also be suspended): These can be used whether the hazard is Category 1 or Category 2. They should, among other things, set out: the nature of the hazard and how the residential premises are affected by it; the deficiency(ies) giving rise to the hazard; the premises on which the hazard arises; the nature of the remedial action; the dates when the remedial action is to be started and when it has to be completed.

- *Emergency Remedial Action*[24] (where there is an **imminent risk of serious harm**): Here, by definition, there must be a Category 1 hazard, and the LHA can take action to remove the imminent risk and then serve the notice (and can recover the costs of taking the action). Having removed the immediate risk, there may still be a Category 1 hazard. There are two key factors to be borne in mind: the risk has to be **imminent**, and the potential harm has to be **serious**.[25]

- *Prohibition Orders*[26] (which may also be suspended): These may prohibit use of any specified premises or of any part of those premises. Prohibition may apply either for all purposes or for any particular purpose (except as may be approved by the LHA). The prohibition can apply to the occupation of the premises as a whole or to a part. It can restrict their use to a particular number of households or persons or prohibit use by a particular category of persons. The order must also include information on rights of appeal and what action or works would be needed for the order to be revoked.

- *Emergency Prohibition Order*[27] (where there is imminent risk of serious harm): This again could be used to remove people from premises where there is an imminent risk of serious harm; so it only applies where there is a Category 1 hazard.
- *Hazard Awareness Notice:*[28] This notice only advises the person on whom it is served of the existence of a Category 1 or Category 2 hazard on the residential premises concerned. It alerts the person to any deficiency(ies) arising from the hazard. It is only advisory and does not create any potential offence for non-compliance, nor can it be appealed.
- *Demolition Order:*[29] Only available where there is a Category 1 hazard.
- *Clearance Area:*[30] Only available where all the dwellings in the area have a Category 1 hazard.

5.38 No Improvement Notices, Prohibition Orders, Hazard Awareness Notices, or other action can be served, made, or taken where there is an Interim or Final Management Order in force. This is because the LHA will be the person having control of the premises.

5.39 Where an Improvement Notice or Prohibition Order is suspended, the suspension must be reviewed at least annually. Improvement Notices and Prohibition Orders are registered as local land charges, but not Hazard Awareness Notices as they merely advise the person served as to the existence of a Category 1 or Category 2 hazard. Other than with the Hazard Awareness Notice, an offence is committed if the notice or order is not complied with in the time given.

Drafting notices

5.40 Whatever provision under Part 1 of the Housing Act is used, including a Hazard Awareness Notice or a Prohibition Order, the notice must include the premises where the hazards arise. An Improvement Notice must specify, in relation to the hazard (or each of the hazards), whether it is a Category 1 or a Category 2 hazard. The same notice can deal with either or both Categories, but it should make this clear. In addition, the notice must set out the deficiencies that have been identified as giving rise to the hazard(s). The notice must also set out what remedial action is to be taken in respect of the hazard(s) and the nature of that remedial action, which need not be limited to "works". The notice must include the date when the remedial action is to commence (no sooner than twenty-eight days from the date of service) and the period within which the remedial action is to be completed. Where there are different timescales for different hazards, these should be clearly stated in the notice.

5.41 The notice must contain information about rights of appeal, the period within which appeals should be made, and where to lodge the appeal (the relevant office of the Tribunal for the region where the property is located). Improvement Notices become operative twenty-one days after service (the appeal period). The LHA has to revoke an Improvement Notice once it is complied with. If there are parts to the notice with different periods for dealing with the hazards, then revocation should be in accordance with those timings.

5.42 Where a notice fails to include all the statutory requirements and it is plain that the notice omitted them, it becomes a nullity, so defective that it cannot be cured by amendment. This could be the result if a notice fails to specify the actual works to be carried out and only states the effect or result to be obtained by the notice.[31] This does not prevent alternative works being accepted after service of an Improvement Notice, which can be varied accordingly.

5.43 A Prohibition Order must include similar information to an Improvement Notice, so that the recipient understands what needs to be done for the order to be revoked.

Power to charge

5.44 Local housing authorities have the power to impose a reasonable charge for recovering administrative and other expenses incurred in determining whether their action is justified, deciding what action to take and for carrying out that decision. This power is available with respect to all the options other than Demolition Orders and Clearance Areas. There is no prescribed maximum charge, but costs need to be reasonable and have to be justified. Local authorities need to consider how best to structure these costs, with hourly rates being charged appropriate to the level of staff involved rather than using a fixed rate. The costs of inspection, of considering the most appropriate action, and for service of the notice can be included. The charge by itself cannot be appealed but can form part of any appeal against a notice or order and could be the main reason why the owner has appealed.

Which course of action?

5.45   Matters that should be considered when deciding which course of action available in Part 1 of the Housing Act 2004 is most appropriate for addressing the hazard and securing a remedy include:

- hazard score (the severity of potential risk);
- housing strategy and strategies on such matters as fuel poverty, energy efficiency, and tackling "rogue" landlords;
- whether member(s) of the vulnerable age group are currently in occupation (it should only be at this stage of the process that the actual occupiers are taken into consideration; thus, different courses of action can be taken for dwellings with hazards of a similar rating but taking into account whether or not the vulnerable age group is in occupation);
- whether the current occupier is vulnerable for other reasons, e.g. disability or ill health;
- need for the same type of property as the subject property in the locality;
- social exclusion and the possibility of lack of access to housing;
- whether the property is empty;
- turnover of tenancies (so it might be appropriate to suspend a notice until there is a change of tenant);
- the views of the owner and the occupiers (in the former case, this might have been indicated earlier in the process, such as when notice of the inspection had been given; for the latter, some discussion should be held at the time of the inspection);
- the proportionality of action given the extant risks;
- practicability of remedying the hazard;
- whether the premises are a listed building.

Fire

5.46   If the hazard identified is that of fire (as defined in the Regulations) in an HMO or the common parts of a building containing flats, then, before taking any enforcement action, the LHA must consult with the fire and rescue authority for the area. Where emergency measures are proposed, this duty to consult applies only so far as it is reasonably practicable to do so. Local authorities and the Fire and Rescue Services should normally have an agreed approach and work to a protocol, particularly where there is the potential for an overlap of powers. For high-rise residential buildings clad with Aluminium Composite Material (ACM), an addendum to the hazard profile for fire has been prepared and was tabled in Parliament (as statutory guidance) on 29 November 2018.[32]

Statement of reasons

5.47   A statement of reasons is required under s.8 of the Housing Act 2004 setting out why a particular course of action has been taken. This has to accompany every notice or order and any copy. A copy of any notice or order must be served on everyone who the LHA knows has an interest in or occupies the dwelling. That is, tenants must receive copies of all notices. It should be noted that tenants have a right of appeal in the case of a Prohibition Order.

5.48   The statement should make it clear why a particular course of action has been taken and should contain reasons, so that the recipient fully understands why the course of action has been taken. The statement can also and perhaps should include any deficiencies and hazards that are not required to be remedied. It should include a reference to any relevant local authority policy such as on enforcement. A tick box approach does not really satisfy the requirements for a properly worded statement. It should be seen as another means of communicating with owners (and tenants), and, when precisely drafted, it could reduce the chances of an appeal.

Use of the enforcement powers

5.49   One of the authors has prepared a report based on responses from local authorities to a Freedom of Information request from Karen Buck MP.[33] Some 255 responses were received from local authorities. Improvement Notices were the most common form of action taken under Part 1 of the Housing Act 2004. Table 5.2 provides some basic

Table 5.2 Improvement notices served

	2014/15	2015/16	2016/17
"0" notices	54	49	49
Total	3181	3570	3366
Maximum served by any LHA	312	411	292
Average*	12	14	13
Median	3	4	5

*Rounded to nearest whole number. Between 58 and 59 respondents left at least one year blank, and between 9 and 12 could not provide the information either with N/K (not kept) or N/A (not readily available).

information on the number of Improvement Notices served. It should be noted that this question asked for notices served including both Category 1 and Category 2 hazards, that is, regardless of whether they were served under s.11 or s.12 of the Housing Act 2004.

5.50 The maximum number of Improvement Notices served by any single authority was 411, in 2015/16. In 2016/17, the maximum served by a single authority was 292. This indicates that, by comparison with the number of dwellings with serious hazards, taking formal action is rare for many local authorities. Less use is made of Prohibition Orders, with the median number made in each of the years 2014/15 to 2016/17 being one – so half of all authorities did not make such an order. The picture was similar for Hazard Awareness Notices, with half of all local authorities not serving any. This result is surprising, given that this is the gentlest option and that non-compliance is not an offence. From a local authority point of view, it is also the easiest option to utilise as there is no appeal provision. A Hazard Awareness Notice does provide an opportunity to escalate the intervention should the recipient fail to remedy the hazard.

5.51 The argument is sometimes put forward that improvements can be achieved by other ways than through enforcement (though outcomes seem not to be well measured). It could be argued that this reflects a lack of confidence in utilising a legal process, either by managers or by the officers themselves. Many officers use "informal" action, e.g. a letter to notify a landlord of deficiencies, and it is only when this does not elicit a positive response that consideration is given to formal action. That leaves tenants vulnerable to retaliatory eviction or, at best, living in hazardous conditions longer than is necessary. This raises at least two points. First, how do officers know that a landlord will turn out to be compliant and co-operative, without wasting time in negotiations? Secondly, if local authorities eschew using formal enforcement measures, the worst or criminal landlords will be unregulated and left free to continue in that way. Reliance on informal methods also means that local authorities will not have access to the provisions on civil penalties, which can help provide additional funding for use in dealing with housing conditions.

5.52 The First-tier Tribunal has made the point that where a Category 1 hazard exists, the local authority should take one of the courses of action set down in the Housing Act 2004 and negotiate afterwards. See, for example, a case involving LB of Wandsworth, where Mr NK Nicol (Tribunal chair) pointed out that the authority took over twenty months to take formal action, having been in negotiations during that period. He added, in relation to Category 1 hazards, that it is unlawful to delay acting:

> *The laudable aim of achieving better outcomes by agreement may be achieved under the Act by delaying enforcement of a notice after service, not before. . . . It does not assist the Appellants to point out that the Respondent may have acted unlawfully in failing to take action in the past.*[34]

5.53   Also in the First-tier Tribunal, LB Southwark was criticised for the approach it took to enforcement and the way a complaint was dealt with. Even though the appeal was lost, the judge found that "the evidence would seem to indicate that the Respondent might have been too indulgent in its dealings with the Applicant". It was of some concern "that the Respondent spent quite so long negotiating with the Applicant on the basis of informal schedules of works".[35]

Civil penalties

5.54   Local housing authorities are able to impose a civil penalty as an alternative to prosecution for certain offences under the Housing Act 2004 and the Housing and Planning Act 2016. Civil penalties are most relevant for a failure to comply with an Improvement Notice – s.30 of the Housing Act 2004.

5.55   The maximum penalty that can be imposed is £30,000 per offence. The size of the penalty has to be determined by the local authority on a case-by-case basis having regard to guidance issued by the MHCLG.[36] Where a landlord fails to comply with an Improvement Notice and subsequently receives a civil penalty as a result, the guidance suggests that a further Improvement Notice could then be issued if the work still has not been carried out. This implies that the first Improvement Notice has to be revoked. In these circumstances, it might be worth carrying out the necessary works in default, based on the requirements of the subsequent notice.

5.56   The same criminal standard of proof is required for a civil penalty as for prosecution. So, before deciding on what action to take, a local housing authority should be satisfied that there is sufficient evidence to support taking a prosecution, with a realistic chance of conviction in the magistrates' court. That means being able to establish beyond reasonable doubt that the offence has been committed. The same standard of proof applies where a civil penalty is imposed and an appeal is subsequently made to the First-tier Tribunal. The full procedure to be followed is set out in the guidance from MHCLG.[37]

5.57 Civil penalties are not available where the local authority has taken action using the statutory nuisance provisions in the EPA 1990 and the person served has failed to comply with an abatement notice.

Works in default

5.58 Where there has been a failure to comply with an Improvement Notice or reasonable progress has not been made carrying out remedial action, LHAs have the power to carry out works in default. Such a power exists independently from prosecution (or imposing a civil penalty). There is also provision to carry out works in default by agreement. In such cases, it would be possible to carry out any work before expiry of the notice.[38]

5.59 In 2009/10, 60% of local authorities said they had not done any work in default (or could not say whether they had or not). In 2016/17, it was reported following the 2017 Freedom of Information request that 77% of local authorities never undertook work in default where there had been a failure to comply with a notice under Part 1 of the Housing Act 2004[39] (around 74% in 2013/14).[40] Given the small number of prosecutions, it would seem that notices had either been complied with or went unenforced.

5.60 Given the current government's desire to crack down on the worst criminal landlords, local authorities should have developed a coherent policy on works in default as part of their enforcement policy and private rented sector strategy. These policies should include such matters as how the decision to carry out works in default is made and the circumstances in which the use of discretion is applicable. The executive decision to carry out works in default should be properly recorded.[41]

5.61 The Battersby Report on local housing authority action on conditions in rented housing not only shows that Improvement Notices are rarely being served but reflects the reality that works in default of compliance will rarely be required.[42] The report found that 187 out of 244 respondents (77%) said that they had never undertaken work in default for failure to comply with a notice under Part 1 of the Housing Act 2004. In the three years to 2016/17, the average number of occasions per year when work in default was utilised was 187. Most local authorities never used Emergency Remedial Action either, and the average number of occasions per year that this course of action was taken, in the same three years, was 185. While at least 90% of local authorities never use this power, one authority used it on twelve occasions in year 2016/17.

5.62   Reports in the media often refer to the lack of prosecutions. This may be an indication of weak enforcement, with few notices being served. But the picture is complicated because, if many of the notices served are complied with, one would expect there to be few prosecutions. Compliance results in the properties involved being made safer and/ or healthier, and this must be the primary aim of regulation.

5.63   What is of greater concern is that too many LHAs are dealing with landlords who want to comply, whilst the worst or criminal landlords (those least compliant with legal requirements and seeking to avoid contact with regulators) are not being identified or being dealt with appropriately. This leaves vulnerable tenants even more exposed to risk from poor conditions.

Recovery of expenses and land charges

5.64   Expenses reasonably incurred can be recovered from the person served with the Improvement Notice – the relevant person. Where the relevant person receives the rent of the premises as agent or trustee for another person, these expenses are also recoverable (wholly or in part) by the authority from that other person. The procedure for enabling local housing authorities to recover expenses reasonably incurred is included in Schedule 3 of the 2004 Act. Expenses can be recovered where the person served with a notice of intention to carry out the works complies with the notice before the work can be done by the local authority.[43] A notice of intention is not required when the work is carried out by agreement.

5.65   Once the demand for payment has been served and has become operative (after any appeal to the First-tier Tribunal has been determined or the period allowed for appeal of twenty-one days has passed), then the sum demanded becomes a charge on the premises. The local authority should enter an enforceable charge on the local land charges register. The demand for payment must be served as soon as possible on the correct person. Fees can be charged, and also interest will accrue from date of service until payment.[44] The sum charged can include a reasonable amount for administrative fees. Fourteen or 15% seems to be a fair amount charged by authorities using this procedure. In a case before the First-tier Tribunal, a 30% administration charge was judged to be excessive.[45]

5.66   An action to recover the costs can start once the demand for payment has become operative. This could include requiring tenants to pay rent to the local authority rather than to the landlord.[46] To achieve this, the authority has to serve a recovery notice on the occupier, which has the effect of transferring to the authority the right to recover and receive the rent. Local authorities may also make use of the services of a specialist debt recovery agent, but such arrangements should be included in their private sector housing policy document.

5.67 The Law of Property Act 1925 applies when the demand for payment becomes operative and a local land charge is placed on the property. The effect of the charge is that the local housing authority has the same powers and remedies available as if it were a mortgagee by deed. Thus, it has powers of sale and leasing, of accepting a surrender of a lease and of appointing a receiver. A receiver can be appointed one month after the charge takes effect. The debt can also be recovered by enforced sale, and a number of local housing authorities have found this to be a good way of recovering the debt. However, the enforced sale process will be halted if the owner of the property pays the council the amount it is owed (and the smaller the charge, the more likely this is to happen).

5.68 The process is similar where the local housing authority chooses to take Emergency Remedial Action, as the authority incurs costs in removing the imminent risk of serious harm. The costs incurred are then claimed by way of a demand for payment. In all cases, the correct procedure has to have been followed and valid notices served in the first place. Otherwise, the demand for payment could be appealed successfully.

Notes

1 SI 2002/1860.
2 Letter of 17 May 2018 from Rt Hon James Brokenshire MP, Secretary of State for Housing Communities and Local Government to all Local Housing Authority Chief Executives. Available at https://assets.publishing.service.gov.uk/ government/uploads/system/uploads/attachment_data/file/707813/Direction_ to_local_authority_chief_executives_17_May_2018.pdf
3 MHCLG/BSP/Advice Note/11/280218. Available at: https://assets.publishing. service.gov.uk/government/uploads/system/uploads/attachment_data/file/684350/ 20180228_-_Update_and_consolidated_advice_for_building_owners_following_ large-scale_testing.pdf
4 See, for example, in Case LON/00AG/HIN/2007/009 – LB Camden, where an Improvement Notice was quashed.
5 See, for example, Case LON/00BE/HPO/2013/0021 and LB Southwark, where the landlord and LHA were already in discussions about licensing; and Case CAM/38UC/HIN/2013/0007, involving Oxford City Council, where the notice of entry was sent to the company to whom rent was paid, but the owner was another company.
6 Management of Houses in Multiple Occupation (England) Regulations 2006. SI 2006/272.
7 *Housing – Fire Safety: Guidance on Fire Safety Provisions for Certain Types of Existing Housing* (London: LACORS, 2008).

8   MAN/00BU/HEP/2013/0001, Trafford Borough Council (29 Foxglove Drive WA14 5JX).

9   *Regulators' Code*, Better Regulation Delivery Office, HM Government: Department for Business, Innovation and Skills, April 2014.

10   *Ibid.*, para 1.1.

11   Regulatory Enforcement and Sanctions Act 2008 (Amendment of Schedule 3) Order 2013, SI 2013 No 2215.

12   *Retaliatory Eviction and the Deregulation Act 2015: A Guidance Note on the Changes Coming into Force on 1 October 2015* (HM Government: DCLG, October 2015), p 10.

13   Deregulation Act 2015, s.34(1).

14   *Ibid.*, s.34(2).

15   *R v Bristol CC ex p. Everett* [1999] 1 WLR 1170. See ch 4.20–4.26.

16   SI 2005 No 3208; in Wales, SI 2006 No 1702 (W.164).

17   Case Ref MAN/36UC/HIN/2010/ 0023.

18   *R (on the application of Vella) v Lambeth London Borough Council* [2005] EWHC 2473 (Admin).

19   Housing Health and Safety Rating System (England) Regulations 2005; Housing Health and Safety Rating System (Wales) Regulations 2006.

20   During the Report Stage of the Homes (Fitness for Human Habitation) Bill in the House of Commons, it was announced by the Parliamentary Undersecretary of State for Housing, Communities and Local Government (Mrs Heather Wheeler) that the operation of the HHSRS would be reviewed in 2019 (Hansard, HC 26 October 2018, Col 553).

21   Chartered Institute of Environmental Health, "HHSRS – 11 Years On". Available at: www.cieh.org/media/1166/hhsrs-11-years-on.pdf

22   For example, there is the RHE Housing Health International Research Bulletin (www.housinghealth.com); also, useful information is in: WHO, *WHO Housing and Health Guidelines* (Geneva, 2018). Available at: http://apps.who.int/iris/bitstream/handle/10665/276001/9789241550376-eng.pdf?ua=1

23   Housing Act 2004, ss.11–19.

24   *Ibid.*, ss.40–42.

25   On this, see comments of the President of the Upper Tribunal (Lands Chamber) in *Bolton MBC v Amratlal Patel* [2010] UKUT 334 (LC) LT Case Number: HA/6/2009. Available at: http://landschamber.decisions.tribunals.gov.uk//judgmentfiles/j727/HA-6-2009.pdf

26   Housing Act 2004, ss.20–27.

27   *Ibid.*, ss.43,44.

28   *Ibid.*, ss.28,29.

29   *Ibid.*, s.46, amending s.265 of the Housing Act 1985.

30   *Ibid.*, s.47, amending s.289 of the Housing Act 1985.

31   *Canterbury City Council v Bern* [1981] JPL 749 (Divisional Court).

32   *HHSRS Operating Guidance. Addendum for the Profile for the Hazard of Fire in Relation to Cladding Systems on High Rise Residential Buildings.* Available at: https://assets.publishing.service.gov.uk/government/uploads/system/uploads/attachment_data/file/760150/Housing_Health_and_Safety_Rating_System_WEB.pdf

33   Battersby S, *Local Housing Authority Action on Conditions in Rented Housing* (2017). Available at: www.sabattersby.co.uk/documents/KB_FoI_2017_Report_Final.pdf

34   Case ref. LON/OOBJ/HIN/2012/0032, *Virdee v London Borough of Wandsworth*.

35 Case ref. LON/00BE/HIN/2015/0005, *Hadjimina v London Borough of South-wark*, per Judge Korn.
36 This is available at: https://assets.publishing.service.gov.uk/government/uploads/system/uploads/attachment_data/file/697644/Civil_penalty_guidance.pdf
37 *Ibid.*
38 Housing Act 2004, sch 3.
39 *Ibid.*
40 Battersby S, *The Challenge of Tackling Unsafe and Unhealthy Housing: Report of a Survey of Local Authorities for Karen Buck MP* (2015). Available at: www.sabattersby.co.uk/documents/KBReport2.pdf
41 Local Authorities (Executive Arrangements) (Meetings & Access to Information) (England) Regulations 2012.
42 See note 37.
43 Housing Act 2004, sch 3, para 4.
44 *Ealing LBC v El Isaac* [1980] 1 WLR 932.
45 See the decision in LON/00AN/HED/2011/0002.
46 Housing Act 2004, sch 3, para 12(2).

6 Statutory nuisance

Procedural and practice issues

Introduction

6.01 Statutory nuisance enforcement has its own set of procedures, which are set down in Part III of the Environmental Protection Act 1990. Provisions for summary proceedings brought by local authorities in England and Wales are provided in ss.80 and 81 of the Act. Scotland is also included, with some variations. Some general provisions in the EPA 1990 are also relevant to statutory nuisance enforcement, such as:

s.157 – Offences by bodies corporate;
s.159 – Application to Crown;
s.160 – Service of notices.

Prosecutions by "persons aggrieved" by statutory nuisances are provided in s.82 of the Act. Equivalent statutory nuisance provisions for Northern Ireland are provided by Part 7 of the Clean Neighbourhoods and Environment Act (Northern Ireland) 2011.

6.02 The Statutory Nuisance (Appeals) Regulations 1995 (as amended)[1] provide for the grounds of appeal for those served with abatement notices. Schedule 3 of the EPA 1990 sets down additional requirements in the *Statutory Nuisances: Supplementary Provisions*. These cover: appeals to magistrates' courts (to the sheriff in Scotland), including the requirement to state the rights of appeal in abatement notices; powers of entry and offences relating to entry; default powers, where a local authority is in default in exercising its statutory duty to cause its area to be inspected to detect any statutory nuisances; protection from personal liability for members and officers of local authorities.

Duty to serve an abatement notice

6.03 Two duties are placed on local authorities triggering statutory nuisance enforcement action. Section 79(1) EPA 1990 provides that:

> *it shall be the duty of every local authority to cause its area*
> *to be inspected from time to time to detect any statutory nui-*
> *sances* . . . *and, where a complaint of a statutory nuisance is*
> *made to it by a person living within its area, to take such steps*
> *as are reasonably practicable to investigate the complaint.*

These two duties cannot be subsumed into a single duty limited to investigating complaints from residents.[2] Local authorities who confine their activity to only investigating complaints from residents or only taking enforcement action in cases where there is more than one complainant are giving themselves a discretion they are not entitled to give. Policies which limit activity in this way or ones that fetter discretion are unlawful[3] and liable to be investigated by the Local Authority Ombudsman.

6.04   The first duty – to inspect for statutory nuisances – is a positive duty that was drafted in order to ensure that local authorities carry out their responsibilities conscientiously.[4] In practice, most enforcement actions originate from complaints made by residents under the second duty, requiring the council to investigate their complaints. A local authority would be entitled to decide that, having investigated the matter, there is no statutory nuisance and therefore no obligation to serve a notice. This would leave a complainant with the option of pursuing their complaint as a "person aggrieved" under s.82 of the EPA 1990.

6.05   The decision by the local authority that a statutory nuisance exists or is likely to occur or recur places it under an obligation to serve an abatement notice.[5] This duty under s.80(1) of the EPA 1990 leaves it with no discretion whether to serve a notice once it is satisfied that a statutory nuisance has arisen. This situation makes it essential for local authorities to have before them sufficient evidential grounds before deciding to serve an abatement notice. This is the most crucial stage in undertaking enforcement action in statutory nuisance cases. It should be made in a considered and proper way once all the relevant evidence is before the decision maker. Officers conducting inspections that may or may not lead to the decision by the local authority that a statutory nuisance situation has arisen need to be very careful at that early stage to avoid concluding that a statutory nuisance exists and noting down that view in a notebook. Otherwise, should a case come before the court, a question may arise over why the abatement notice had not been served as soon as reasonably practicable after the time of the entry in the officer's notebook.[6]

6.06   In cases of noise nuisance from premises, under s.79(1)(g) EPA 1990, the local authority has a power to delay service of the abatement notice for up to seven days, if it has reason to believe that some alternative course of action is likely to be effective in persuading the responsible person to abate the nuisance.[7] The alternative action could be taken under some other statutory remedy, such as serving a notice under the Noise Act 1996 or using powers provided by the Anti-social Behaviour, Crime and Policing Act 2014. The alternative action has to be decided upon within the seven-day period rather than the nuisance problem having to be resolved within that time.[8] This would suggest that the power to delay service of the abatement notice could be used in a relatively complex noise nuisance case which requires that steps or works need to be carried out rather than a stipulation in the notice simply to abate the nuisance. "Some alternative action" is not further defined in the legislation, so arguably, in a noisy neighbour dispute, it could include making a referral to a community mediation scheme.

6.07   The decision that an abatement notice needs to be served on the person (or persons) responsible for a statutory nuisance is very important and should only be made once the supporting evidence is sufficient to justify taking this step. The "person responsible" is defined in s.79(7) of the EPA 1990 as "the person to whose act, default or sufferance the nuisance is attributable". An "act" implies a positive intervention; "default" implies a failure to perform a required act; and "sufferance" implies that the person responsible has tolerated the nuisance or has allowed it to happen. Where a nuisance arises from any defect of a structural character, the owner of the premises is the person responsible.[9] "Owner" is not defined in the EPA 1990: It may be the freeholder in a purpose-built block of flats, or a long leaseholder, or the head leaseholder. The person having the responsibility for maintaining the structure of the building would be the person responsible in this situation.

Form of the abatement notice

6.08   The local authority has a duty to serve a notice under s.80(1) of the EPA 1990:

> *imposing all or any of the following requirements –*
>
> (a)   *requiring the abatement of the nuisance or prohibiting or restricting its occurrence or recurrence;*
>
> (b)   *requiring the execution of such works, and the taking of such other steps, as may be necessary for any of those purposes.*

6.09   The words "all or any" indicate that the local authority can choose which requirements to set down in the notice. It has a wide discretion whether to serve a specific works notice or a simple abatement notice.[10] If the former is served, then the local authority must specify the works clearly, so that there is no ambiguity as to what is required of the person served with the notice.[11]

6.10 Although case law has maintained that councils have a wide discretion to serve simple abatement notices, serving such notices does not always amount to good practice. It cannot be good practice if the recipient of the notice is left wondering what he or she needs to do to avoid breaching it. This would be the case with unclear or ambiguous drafting or where the recipient receives a simple notice meant to control a complex problem. In complex statutory nuisance cases, it will usually constitute good practice for precise requirements to be stipulated rather than to rely on a simple abatement form of notice. This need for precision particularly applies for statutory nuisances arising from the state of premises – s.79(1)(a) EPA 1990 – or where the source of the nuisance is from industrial, trade, or business premises.

6.11 Premises that have fallen into a state of disrepair will usually come under the health limb of s.79(1)(a) EPA 1990.[12] In most cases, the responsibility for repairs falls on the landlord, and the person suffering the statutory nuisance is the tenant. Although it probably would be lawful to serve a simple abatement notice on the landlord in this situation, it would be more practical and effective if the notice specified clearly and in some detail what needs to be done to resolve the problem.

6.12 Good practice suggests that complex statutory nuisance cases are better resolved when clear and precise requirements are specified in abatement notices. Written guidance will often be useful in assisting with drafting. Such guidance may originate from government sources or from industry or professional bodies.[13] Although generally not legally binding, relevant good practice documents are sources of advice which officers should be aware of and need to have regard to.

6.13 It is unusual for the courts to make evaluative comments about good practice, though they may question the competence of officers if published guidance has not been followed. In *Brentwood Borough Council v City and Country (Warley) Ltd* (2009) – an unreported (and non-binding) Crown Court appeal concerning the validity of a s.60 Control of Pollution Act 1974 construction site noise notice – the court was highly critical of the approach taken by the local authority. The notice had been drafted without regard to any published guidance and was a standard form of notice that had been used by the council over several decades. The council's policy was to use standard conditions for notices without consideration being given to the specific circumstances of the construction site in question. The presiding judge in *Brentwood BC*, HHJ Saggerson, was highly critical of the approach taken by the local authority; and emphasised [at para. 17] that: "reasonableness and proportionality affect the extent or scope of any Notice (that is to say its impact on the works in question and the recipient of the Notice) and also the manner and terms in which the Notice is drafted". The learned judge went on to affirm a fundamental principle that applies generally to enforcement notices:

> *Any Notice must have precision and clarity; bring about certainty and thus have unambiguous enforcement boundaries. Criminal sanctions can follow from any breach.*

6.14   A local authority is not obliged to consult with the person believed to be responsible for the statutory nuisance over the form of the abatement notice it intends to serve. It is good practice to consult as it demonstrates that a fair and proportionate response is being taken by the council. Further, a ground for appealing an abatement notice is where the local authority is believed to have "refused unreasonably to accept compliance with alternative requirements, or that the requirements of the abatement notice are otherwise unreasonable in character or extent, or are unnecessary".[14] Succeeding on this ground of appeal is unlikely where proper consultation has taken place with the intended recipient.

6.15   It is also good practice to consult when a problem arises on industrial, trade, or business premises, where a best practicable means (BPM) defence is available. A person served with an abatement notice where BPM is available may appeal on the ground that BPM "were used to prevent, or to counteract the effects of, the nuisance".[15] This ground for appealing the notice is an important reason why investigating officers should be prepared to explore with businesses whether BPM have been used to mitigate the nuisance.

6.16   Consultation will not always be feasible. It might be the case that there is a need for urgent action because of a health risk or because the alleged perpetrator is not amenable to a consultation.

Appeals

6.17   The recipient of an abatement notice may appeal to a magistrates' court[16] to have it quashed or to have the requirements varied to make them less onerous.[17] The appeal is a civil matter which is commenced by way of making a complaint to the court.[18] The local authority becomes the defendant in an action brought by the person served with the notice, who is the appellant. The grounds for appealing the notice need to be specified and are set down in the Statutory

Nuisance (Appeals) Regulations 1995 (as amended).[19] All relevant grounds of appeal should be included. If there is doubt as to whether a particular ground is relevant, it should be included. It can subsequently be withdrawn if the appellant decides not to pursue the point at the hearing, in which case it should be withdrawn as early as possible to avoid wasting legal costs or the court's time.

6.18 The appeal should be lodged with the court within twenty-one days of the date of service of the abatement notice.[20] Time begins to run from the date when the recipient was properly served with the notice, not from the date on which the local authority issued it. The court does not have an express power to extend the time limit for appeal; neither should such a power be implied.[21]

6.19 The purpose of bringing an appeal is to test the local authority's justification for serving the abatement notice. The time when the court has to consider this is the date on which the notice was served, not the date of the court hearing.[22] The court hearing an appeal should be considering the validity of the notice, not whether a breach of the notice has occurred. The court is concerned about such matters as whether the threshold for statutory nuisance has been reached and whether the notice was drafted in the correct form, free from mistake or ambiguity, and then properly served on the right person or persons.

6.20 The effect of bringing an appeal will sometimes be that a notice is suspended until either the appeal has been abandoned or has been decided by the court. There are strictly limited situations where suspension is applicable. The grounds set out in regulation 3(1) of the Statutory Nuisance (Appeals) Regulations 1995 for suspending a notice are:

- either because compliance would involve expenditure in carrying out works before the appeal is heard; or
- in the case of noise nuisances (under ss.79(1)(g) or (ga) of the EPA 1990), such noise is necessarily caused in the performance of some duty imposed by law on the appellant.

6.21 Where either of these grounds is met, suspension of a notice does **not** apply where the nuisance:

- is injurious to health; or
- is likely to be of limited duration such that suspension would render the notice of no practical effect; or
- the expenditure in carrying out works required by the notice before any appeal has been decided would not be disproportionate to the public benefit to be expected in that period from compliance.[23]

6.22   When a local authority serves an abatement notice and wishes to invoke suspension, it must include in the body of the notice:

- a statement that it is not suspended pending the appeal; and
- the relevant regulation that applies (regulation 3(2)); and
- the grounds in regulation 3(2) on which the local authority is relying.[24]

6.23   A number of grounds of appeal are set out in regulation 2(2) of the Statutory Nuisance (Appeals) Regulations 1995. Any one or more of these grounds need to be stipulated in the notice of appeal lodged with the court, which then forms the complaint against the local authority. The appellant is not required to give detailed particulars of each ground of appeal at this stage.

6.24   The magistrates' court in exercising its civil jurisdiction does have case management powers to ensure that cases are properly prepared in advance of the final hearing.[25] These powers can be invoked by the parties or by the court to ensure that the evidence forming the basis for the local authority's decision to serve the abatement notice is served on the appellant before the hearing and filed with the court. Further, a direction can be made requiring the appellant to serve detailed grounds of their appeal on the local authority and to file them with the court, including any evidence to be relied on at the final hearing. If case management decisions are not agreed between the parties, then an application can be made to the court at a preliminary hearing to make them compulsory.

6.25   On hearing the appeal, the court may:

- quash the abatement notice to which the appeal relates; or
- vary the notice in favour of the appellant in such manner as it thinks fit; or
- dismiss the appeal.

The effect of the court making an order varying a notice is that the notice "shall have effect as though it had been made by the local authority".[26] It would appear that the court does not have a general power to amend or vary a notice, such as during a preliminary hearing of the appeal, or to add a third party. The power to vary or amend the notice only applies at the end of the hearing in accordance with regulation 2(5)(b).[27]

6.26   Either party may appeal, without leave, to the Crown Court against any decision of the magistrates' court.[28] The procedures set down in the Crown Court Rules on appeals apply to all types of appeal against the magistrates' decision, whether civil or criminal.[29] Notification of the appeal and of the grounds must be made within twenty-one days of the date of the decision in the magistrates' court.[30] The recipient of a notice cannot introduce fresh grounds of appeal but may appeal to the Crown Court on selected grounds from his or her previous appeal to the magistrates.

6.27 The Crown Court appeal, which will be a rehearing, is heard by a judge sitting with two magistrates. Because it is a rehearing, the court will be free to assess the facts anew, and the parties will not be confined to presenting their evidence in the same way as earlier in the magistrates' court. Different or additional evidence may be called by both parties.

Breach of the abatement notice

6.28 Section 80(4) of the EPA 1990 provides as follows:

> *If a person on whom an abatement notice is served, without reasonable excuse, contravenes or fails to comply with any requirement or prohibition imposed by the notice, he shall be guilty of an offence.*

In local authority proceedings under s.80 of the EPA 1990, the prosecutor has to prove, to the criminal standard of proof, that the abatement notice was breached. Where a simple abatement notice has been served under s.80(1)(a), the offence is one of failing, without reasonable excuse, to abate or restrict the nuisance or to have caused, allowed, or permitted the nuisance to occur or recur. It is necessary to prove, therefore, the existence of the nuisance at the time of breach of the notice. In the case of a specific works or steps notice, drafted to include the requirements set out in s.80(1)(b), the offence is one of failing, without reasonable excuse, to comply with the requirements stipulated in the notice. The prosecution's task is simpler where a specific works or steps notice has been served. Breach involves a failure to comply with specific requirements; as s.80(4) makes clear, compliance refers to **any** and not all of the requirements stipulated in the notice.

6.29 For statutory nuisances involving the state of the premises under s.79(1)(a) of the EPA 1990, the abatement notice will usually be drafted to include steps or works that need to be carried out to abate the nuisance within a specified time frame. If any part of a schedule of works is not carried out within the time allowed in the notice, then there will be a breach, subject to the defence of "reasonable excuse".

6.30   Breach of s.80(4) of the EPA 1990 constitutes a criminal offence. The prosecution is required to prove all the elements of the offence to the criminal standard of "beyond reasonable doubt". Section 80(4) also requires proof that an abatement notice was properly served on the defendant. The prosecution also has to prove that there was no "reasonable excuse" for breaching the abatement notice. The burden is initially on the defendant to raise the nature of the excuse. It then falls on the prosecution to prove, beyond reasonable doubt, that the excuse is not reasonable.[31]

6.31   The decision by the local authority whether or not to prosecute for breach of an abatement notice – as with all criminal offences – is an exercise in the use of discretion. Proper and sufficient consideration by the person or persons responsible for making the decision on behalf of the local authority is required. Underlying this decision is a requirement that the evidential test for bringing the prosecution be satisfied before commencement of proceedings. This should be followed by proper consideration being given to the public interest factors. This procedure is stipulated in the *Code for Crown Prosecutors* issued by the Crown Prosecution Service (CPS).[32] No matter how serious the breach or the harm resulting from it, if the evidence is not sufficient to provide a realistic prospect of conviction, then it would be improper to commence or continue with a prosecution.

Best practicable means defence

6.32   A best practicable means (BPM) defence is separate from the defence of having a reasonable excuse to contravene the abatement notice. It is available:

- as a ground of appeal against an abatement notice;[33]
- in a prosecution under s.80(4) of the EPA 1990 for failure to comply with an abatement notice;[34]
- in a prosecution under s.82(8) of the EPA 1990 for failure to comply with an abatement order issued by the magistrates' court under s.82(2) of the EPA 1990.[35]

6.33   A BPM defence is normally only available where the nuisance arises on industrial, trade, or business premises.[36] In a prosecution, the defendant has to prove, to a civil standard of proof, that BPM were used to prevent or counteract the effects of the nuisance.[37] What constitutes BPM is ultimately a decision of the court, though it would be good practice for the prosecutor to take a proper view about whether the defence is likely to succeed.

6.34 The scope of BPM is given a wide interpretation in s.79(9) EPA 1990:

> *"[B]est practicable means" is to be interpreted by reference to the following provisions –*
>
> (*a*) *"practicable" means reasonably practicable having regard among other things to local conditions and circumstances, to the current state of technical knowledge and to the financial implications;*
>
> (*b*) *the means to be employed include the design, installation, maintenance and manner and periods of operation of plant and machinery, and the design, construction and maintenance of buildings and structures;*
>
> (*c*) *the test is to apply only so far as compatible with any duty imposed by law;*
>
> (*d*) *the test is to apply only so far as compatible with safety and safe working conditions, and with the exigencies of any emergency or unforeseeable circumstances.*

Notes

1 SI 1995/2644.
2 Pointing J, Commercial Statutory Nuisances and Loss of Control by Local Authorities, *Environmental Law & Management* Vol. 23 (2011), 333–335.
3 *Anisminic Ltd v Foreign Compensation Commission* [1969] 2 AC 147.
4 This duty originated in the Sanitary Act 1866, s.20.
5 *R v Carrick DC, ex p Shelley* [1996] Env LR 273.
6 In the noise nuisance case of *Hackney LBC v Rottenberg* [2007] EWHC 166 (Admin), investigations were carried out separately by five officers over several months. Four of the officers opined that there had been a statutory nuisance at the time of their visit. This begged the question of why a notice had not been served soon after the first occasion in which that conclusion had been reached rather than delaying service for several months afterwards.
7 EPA 1990, s.80(2A).
8 *Southampton City Council v Odysseas* [2017] EWHC 2783 (Admin).
9 EPA 1990, s.80(2)(b).
10 *R v Falmouth & Truro Port Health Authority, ex p South West Water Ltd* [2000] EWCA Civ 96.
11 *Sterling Homes (Midlands) Ltd v Birmingham City Council* [1996] Env LR 121.
12 See ch 4.13–4.29.
13 Such guidance is often invaluable and authoritative, e.g., *Neighbourhood Noise Policies and Practice for Local Authorities – A Management Guide* (London: DEFRA/CIEH, 2006).

14 Statutory Nuisance (Appeals) Regulations 1995, SI 1995/2644, reg 2(2)(c).
15 *Ibid.*, reg 2(2)(e).
16 EPA 1990, s 80(3). In Scotland, appeal is by summary application to the sheriff.
17 Statutory Nuisance (Appeals) Regulations 1995, SI 1995/2644, reg 2(5).
18 Magistrates' Courts Rules 1981, SI 1981/552, r 34.
19 SI 1995/2644.
20 EPA 1990, s.80(3). Where the last day falls on a Sunday, Good Friday, or Christmas Day, the appeal should be lodged by the day before.
21 *R v Secretary of State for the Environment, ex p Ostler* [1976] 3 All ER 90.
22 *SFI Group plc (formerly Surrey Free Inns plc) v Gosport BC* [1999] Env LR 750.
23 Statutory Nuisance (Appeals) Regulations 1995, SI 1995/2644, reg 3(2).
24 *Ibid.*, reg 3(3).
25 The Magistrates' Courts (Amendment) Rules 2009, SI 2009/3362 amended the Magistrates' Courts Rules 1981 by inserting rule 3A on case management, thereby providing the magistrates' court in its civil jurisdiction with similar powers as in its criminal jurisdiction.
26 Statutory Nuisance (Appeals) Regulations 1995, SI 1995/2644, reg 2(5).
27 *Waveney DC v Lowestoft (North East Suffolk) Magistrates Court* [2008] EWHC 3295 (Admin), para 29.
28 EPA 1990, sch. 3, para 1(3).
29 Crown Court Rules 1982, SI 1982/1109 (as amended).
30 *Ibid.*, r 7.
31 *Polychronakis v Richards & Jerrom Ltd* [1997] EWHC Admin 885.
32 *Code for Crown Prosecutors*, Crown Prosecution Service, 8th ed, 2018.
33 Statutory Nuisance (Appeals) Regulations 1995, reg 2.
34 EPA 1990, s.80(7) and (8).
35 The defence is also probably available in respect of an application for an abatement order under EPA 1990, s.82(2) by a "person aggrieved".
36 EPA 1990, s.80(8). See ch 4.50–4.54, for BPM and noise nuisance.
37 EPA 1990, s.80(7).

7 Other remedies, powers, and related actions

Summary proceedings by persons aggrieved by statutory nuisances: EPA 1990 s.82

7.01 Unlike the Housing Act 2004, s.82 of the Environmental Protection Act 1990 permits any persons affected or "aggrieved" by the existence of a statutory nuisance to take their own action and obtain a nuisance abatement order in the magistrates' court. Other than for matters of disrepair under the Landlord and Tenant Act 1985, this has been the only route by which tenants could seek redress for housing conditions.[1] This changes with the Homes (Fitness for Human Habitation) Act 2018 which adds the HHSRS hazards to the standard of fitness in the 1985 Act and so broadens the scope for action.

7.02 Much of the case law pertaining to statutory nuisances resulting from the state of residential premises – under s.79(1)(a) EPA 1990 – has been the result of persons aggrieved taking their own actions under s.82 EPA 1990 (and its predecessor in s.99 of the Public Health Act 1936).[2] The prejudicial to health limb under s.79(1) is available for internal statutory nuisances, the nuisance limb only being so when a property boundary has been crossed, when neighbouring property is affected.[3]

7.03 Where it alleged that the state of the premises is prejudicial to health, the information and guidance within the HHSRS Operating Guidance may be used to support that contention. As this guidance is based on research evidence, the information contained within some of the hazard profiles can be supportive in statutory nuisance cases. Care must be taken, however, to avoid confusing the two provisions. The guidance will only be relevant for certain kinds of hazard where the risks are to the health of occupiers.

Commencing a prosecution under s.82

7.04 Those directly affected by the statutory nuisance may complain to their local magistrates' court, under s.82 of the EPA 1990. Section

82(7) of the Act requires at least twenty-one days' notice to be given in writing of the intention to complain (in effect seek the issue of a summons) to the magistrates' court and to institute proceedings (this is three days' notice in the case of a noise nuisance). The provisions in s.82 are largely based on those formerly provided in s.99 of the Public Health Act 1936; however, under the earlier legislation, there were no such notice requirements.

7.05   In *Leeds v Islington LBC*,[4] it was made it clear that a notice under s.82(6) must be served at the "proper office" of the prospective defendant. In the case of a corporate body like a local authority, proper service must be to its registered or principal office.[5] The local housing office address (even if that is the address given on the tenant's handbook for complaint) would not be adequate. In the linked appeals of *Hall v Kingston upon Hull CC*, *Ireland v Birmingham CC* and *Baker v Birmingham CC* to the High Court,[6] the tenants had sent the notice to addresses as specified for service in various letters and documents issued by the appropriate local authorities. The prosecutions were subsequently dismissed at first instance on the basis that they had not been properly served at the "proper address". However, the High Court allowed the tenants' appeals. Under s.160(5) EPA 1990, the person to be served has the power to specify an alternative address for service. It was held that in each case the local authority had specified an alternative address, and so "proper service" had been effected. The High Court found that

> *if in any particular local authority area there is uncertainty on the part of either the local authority's tenants or their legal advisers as to where and to whom section 82(6) notices should be sent it seems to us in everyone's interests for the local, authority to inform its tenants precisely how to proceed.*

7.06   The person aggrieved does not have to be in legal occupation at the time of the hearing or, indeed, have to be a tenant. The High Court in *Hall et al.*[7] decided that "whether a complainant is a 'person aggrieved' for the purposes of section 82(1) of the 1990 Act is always a question of fact and degree". It is also true that moving the occupier out does not necessarily mean the premises are no longer a statutory nuisance. It was subsequently held in *Watkins*[8] that it is:

> *not necessarily in every case, sufficient for a complainant to be a "person aggrieved" if the complainant is in actual occupation, whether or not lawful occupation. If the legality of the occupation is a matter of bona fide dispute at the time the*

> *complaint is made, then it is likely, though not axiomatic, that the complainant will be found to be a person aggrieved.*

7.07 There is no prescribed form for the written notice under s.82(6) EPA 1990. Nor is there any prescribed form for drafting the "information" to the magistrates' court, which is the essential step required for the court to issue a summons. It will be necessary to demonstrate why it is considered that a statutory nuisance exists, giving some indication as to the nature of the defects, and why the state of the premises is such as to be prejudicial to health or a nuisance. The information should also include details as to who is responsible for the existence of the statutory nuisance and give their address. In the case of premises where the problems are of a structural nature, the person responsible is the owner, and the information should state this. The information should also set out how the complainant has become a "person aggrieved". The information should include a draft summons that can be issued once the magistrates are satisfied that there is a case to answer. Precedents are available in various publications that will help advisers or those wishing to initiate action.[9]

Proceedings in the magistrates' court

7.08 The proceedings for hearing the summons are criminal, and the criminal burden of proof will apply. The *Criminal Procedure Rules* govern the conduct of the prosecution at every stage.[10] The prosecution has to show beyond reasonable doubt that the defendant is responsible for the existence of the statutory nuisance. If the court is satisfied at the end of the trial that the alleged nuisance exists, they may make an Abatement Order, ordering the defendant to do one or more of the following:

- abate the nuisance within a specified time;
- prohibit its recurrence;
- execute any works necessary to achieve abatement.[11]

The court must be satisfied as to the existence of the statutory nuisance (or its likelihood of recurrence) at the date of the hearing.[12]

7.09 Where the court is satisfied that the statutory nuisance exists and the premises are unfit for human habitation, it may prohibit their residential use until rendered fit to the court's satisfaction. In an action by the tenants of a block of flats, in which it was alleged that the whole block was prejudicial to health, it was held that the only risk to each tenant derived from the condition of their own flat, and so the individual flats constituted the relevant premises, not the whole block.[13]

7.10   On conviction, the court may impose an unlimited fine[14] and may award compensation for damage and injury suffered as a result of the existence of the nuisance. A Compensation Order should be made if the tenant or occupier has suffered damage to the person or to their property. Section 63 of the Legal Aid, Sentencing and Punishment of Offenders Act 2012 requires the court to consider making such an order. There is no limit to the size of the award, nor is it necessary to show that there would be liability in civil proceedings, such as for a breach of the repairing obligation under the Landlord and Tenant Act 1985. However, evidence of actual loss is required.

7.11   Under s.82(12) EPA 1990, the magistrates are bound to make a costs order in favour of the person aggrieved, once they have found that a statutory nuisance existed at the date of making the complaint.[15] If the nuisance was abated after the date of making the complaint but prior to the hearing, then the power to make a costs order under s.82(12) is still available regardless of whether the nuisance is likely to recur.

7.12   Where work is not done in accordance with the Abatement Order, a continuing daily fine may be imposed by the court from the date of conviction. In *Parry v Walsall* (1997),[16] Aldridge and Brownhills magistrates had ordered the council, in May 1996, to carry out works following a successful prosecution under s.82. The work was not done, and the tenant was issued fresh proceedings under s.82(8). At trial, on 15 October 1996, the justices convicted the council and ordered it to complete the original works within a further twenty-one days but imposed no financial penalty. The work was still not done. The tenant issued further s.82(8) proceedings seeking a fine and a continuing daily penalty. The work was finally completed on 4 February 1997. The justices, in basing their decision on the full extent of s.82(8), imposed both a fixed initial fine and a continuing daily fine from the date of conviction, imposing fines totalling £45,000.

Legal cases interpreting the scope of s.82

7.13   When a tenant takes action using s.82 EPA 1990, it is open to the landlord to avoid liability by satisfying the court that he or she is not the person responsible for the nuisance.[17] In *Carr v London Borough of Hackney*,[18] the tenant had argued that the only way to abate the statutory nuisance (condensation and mould growth) and prevent recurrence was for gas central heating to be installed. The stipendiary magistrate acquitted the council, having found that any recurrence would arise from the tenant's failure to allow the council to install electric convector heaters – which it wished to provide – and which the court accepted would be sufficient to abate the statutory nuisance. The tenant appealed, contending that if Parliament had intended such a defence to exist, it would have been explicit in the 1990 Act, as it had been in the previous statutory nuisance provisions of the 1936 Public Health Act. The Divisional Court dismissed the appeal and held that such a defence was obviously available notwithstanding the absence of a specific provision in the 1990 Act.

7.14 In the unreported case of *Ali v Camden LBC* (1996), before Wells Street Magistrates' Court, the council had accepted that the premises were a statutory nuisance by reason of damp and mould growth. It had offered to provide alternative temporary accommodation during the eight weeks of remedial works that would be needed to deal with the problem. The tenant refused two offers of alternative temporary housing. The stipendiary magistrate acquitted the council and awarded it costs out of central funds. The nuisance existed and continued not by default of the council but because of the unreasonable refusal of the tenant to vacate temporarily. This case confirms that there cannot be a conviction unless on the date of the hearing it is the defendant who can be shown to be responsible for the continuing statutory nuisance.[19]

7.15 In *Murphy v Lambeth LBC* (2013),[20] an unreported case heard in Camberwell Magistrates' Court, a top floor flat was affected by damp and mould and the roof space above was uninsulated. An environmental health practitioner confirmed that the state of the premises amounted to a statutory nuisance as they were prejudicial to health. Works that had been recommended to abate the statutory nuisance included upgrading the heating system and carrying out substantial insulation work, including to the walls. These works required the services in the flat to be moved. Advice was given that the works could be done with the tenant in occupation, but they would need to be carefully planned. The defendant wanted to carry out the works, but the tenant was not given reassurances as to how the works would be planned and managed and so refused access. Subsequent attempts by council workers to gain access to wipe down the mould failed because they had turned up without making appointments. Section 82 proceedings were issued. The prosecution was defended by the council on the basis that Murphy had refused access, and this amounted to an abuse of process. Heating records were obtained from the heating supplier, and an expert who inspected them confirmed that the heating system was undersized and that Murphy had been using the heating system properly. Accordingly, the only real defence was over the refusal of access. However, the council pleaded guilty. At trial, the judge did not fine the council but increased the size of damages awarded to Murphy to £4000.[21] This was on the grounds of loss of amenity given the severity of the problem, in that the property was uninhabitable and the damp was all-pervasive, so that it also made the children's clothes smell foully. Works totalling £15,000 were also ordered to be carried out and the defendant ordered to prevent a recurrence of the problem. Since there can be no offence under s.82 unless the statutory nuisance is found to exist on the date of the hearing, the earliest date that compensation can be awarded from will be the date the twenty-one-day notice expires, not the whole period the statutory nuisance existed. The maximum period of inconvenience and distress for which compensation can be claimed is six months.[22]

7.16   In the case of *Earl v Kingston upon Hull* (1996),[23] the tenants alleged that the state of the premises were prejudicial to health arising from condensation mould growth resulting from lack of heating. The council house was fitted with only a single gas fire. Before issue of the summons, the council had removed the mould and applied fungicidal paint. It alleged that the mould had arisen from the tenant's failure to supplement the heating provided. The tenant's independent EHP gave evidence based on electronic temperature and humidity monitoring to show that mould and proliferating dust mites would return and thus the statutory nuisance would recur. The stipendiary magistrate convicted the council, holding that to prevent recurrence, the tenants would be put to "wholly disproportionate effort and expense". The council was ordered to carry out extensive works, including supplying full gas central heating and also had to pay the tenants' prosecution costs.

Criticisms of s.82

7.17   Section 82 EPA 1990 provisions were recently criticised in a report prepared for Shelter by the Law Schools of Bristol and Kent Universities following the Grenfell Tower disaster.[24] The authors accepted, however, that the tenure neutrality of statutory nuisance is a major advantage. They made a number of criticisms. The first was that "this route is not well-trodden ground – although there have in the past been several legal campaigns using the device". Of major concern, they argued, is the lack of legal expertise in this area of law which, combined with the lack of public funding for bringing prosecutions, makes it difficult for occupiers to find lawyers willing to take on cases. The authors maintained that statutory nuisance is a relatively risky avenue to take for any occupier seeking to improve housing conditions. This is exacerbated because Legal Aid is no longer available to an occupier bringing a prosecution, and the criminal burden of proof presents a high evidential hurdle. One lawyer respondent in the study opined:

> *Criminal prosecution in the magistrates' court is the wrong process and the wrong court. The procedure is completely inaccessible to all except a very few people who may be able to find a solicitor willing to take the case under a CFA [conditional fee agreement]. There is a need for expert evidence which will be sufficient to meet the criminal standard of proof. Most magistrates will be completely unaware of their jurisdiction under the EPA, and will need a crash course in what it is about.*

7.18   The authors of the study recommended that the element of statutory nuisance law which relates to housing conditions should be repealed. This recommendation was made subject to new legislation being enacted providing suitable replacement mechanisms for tenants to hold landlords to account for letting unhealthy, unsafe, and unfit premises. The authors were critical of the narrow interpretation of "health" and what is prejudicial to health set down in the case law.[25] The report concluded:

> *In a modern and effective system of regulation that prioritises the health and safety of occupiers, statutory nuisance is anachronistic. Its Victorian roots, the complexity and risks involved in its use, and the fact that it is adjudicated upon by the Magistrates Court which has very limited expertise in housing, make it not fit for purpose.*

7.19   The authors also welcomed the provisions of the Homes (Fitness for Human Habitation) Bill, supported by Karen Buck, MP, concerning new routes for the enforcement by occupiers of the HHSRS and fire safety regulations. This measure will require landlords to ensure that the dwelling is fit for occupation when let and remains so for the duration of the tenancy. It adds the twenty-nine HHSRS hazards to the standard of fitness set down in s.10 of the Landlord and Tenant Act 1985. The dwelling will be not be fit if there are hazards and if the dwelling is not reasonably suitable for occupation. Additionally, the rent limits set in s.8 of the 1985 Act will be removed. Subject to such a measure reaching the Statute Book, the authors of the report recommended repeal of s.82 of the EPA 1990 in respect of housing conditions. Homes (Fitness for Human Habitation) Act 2018 received the Royal Assent in December 2018 and came into force on 20 March 2019. It only applies in England.

7.20 Despite calls for wholesale revision of the law on housing, there is no indication from the government that the housing conditions element of s.82 EPA 1990 will be repealed.[26] Compensation as part of an s.82 action is limited compared to a civil damages claim under the Landlord and Tenant Act 1985 for a breach of a repairing obligation, and presumably this will continue now the Buck Bill has become law. The burden of proof under the Landlord and Tenant Act 1985 is lower than in an s.82 action, where the criminal standard applies. This makes it more difficult for the tenant using s.82 to prove that the landlord is responsible for the damp and mould in the dwelling causing the risk to health. The occupiers inevitably contribute to the high relative humidity, which leads to condensation, mould, and an increase in the house dust mite population. The moisture generated by normal household activities could be 12 litres or more a day, but the issue is whether the dwelling is capable of dealing with it. An investigation in an s.82 action has to be detailed and sufficient to show, beyond reasonable doubt, that the landlord is responsible.

Anti-social behaviour powers

7.21 The Anti-social Behaviour, Crime and Policing Act 2014 provides various powers enabling local authorities, the police, and social landlords to deal with anti-social behaviour (ASB). The aims of this legislation include controlling a wide range of conduct – by individuals or bodies/institutions – that amount to anti-social behaviour and to provide the means for controlling issues that "fall through the gaps" of existing legislative provisions. Regard should be had to Home Office Statutory Guidance[27] and to the advice published by the Chartered Institute of Environmental Health[28] on the use of these powers.

7.22 The measures in the 2014 Act relevant to the use of residential property are Community Protection Notices (CPNs), Closure Notices, and Civil Injunctions. These can be used as ways of controlling behavioural forms of nuisance and lower levels amounting to annoyance, as well as more serious forms of misbehaviour. Causing unreasonable and persistent noise affecting neighbours in residential property is one example, but the range of ASB is wide and this legislation is drafted to accommodate this.

Community Protection Notices

7.23 Community Protection Notices can be issued by authorised council officers, police officers, and social landlords if designated by the council.[29] These notices are intended to deal with repeated or ongoing conduct – not occasional or "one-off" conduct. The test for such conduct is set out in s.43 of the 2014 Act, which requires that the investigating officer is satisfied, on reasonable grounds, that the conduct of the individual or body (a business, company, or other organisation):

- is having a detrimental effect on the quality of life of those in the locality; and
- is unreasonable; and
- the behaviour is of a persistent or continuing nature.

7.24 In deciding whether the conduct complained of is having a sufficiently detrimental effect on the quality of life of those in the local community, investigating officers should base their decisions on evidence. Normally, they should speak to victims to obtain first-hand accounts of the conduct, of its characteristics such as frequency and duration, and of the seriousness and breadth of its impact. Investigating officers should make a record of complainants' accounts. Complainants should be warned that they may be asked to provide a written statement or to give oral evidence in court at a future stage.

7.25 The investigating officer must also make a judgement as to whether the conduct is in itself unreasonable. This implies an objective standard, so what would be unreasonable to the average person in the locality is the test, not whether the complainant believes that the conduct is unreasonable or intolerable. Distinguishing between conduct that is inherently unreasonable and conduct which is exacerbated by extrinsic factors will be important. For instance, where there is poor sound insulation between two properties, it would not be unreasonable to watch television at a moderate volume even though it is audible in a neighbouring home.

7.26 A CPN can be issued in a housing context against those who are responsible for ASB, such as: tenants, occupiers, or other persons, including corporate bodies. Rogue landlords and property agents can also be issued with CPNs, where the s.43 criteria are met. With these cases, if the CPN is breached and the person convicted, a local authority (in England) can apply to the First-tier Tribunal for a banning order under s.15 of the Housing and Planning Act 2016.[30] The effect of this order is that a person could be banned, for a specified length of at least twelve months, from letting housing or engaging in letting agency or property management work.[31]

7.27   A written warning must be issued to the person or body believed to be responsible for the anti-social behaviour prior to issuing a CPN. Where a written warning has not been heeded, a CPN may be issued by an authorised person to an individual (over the age of sixteen) or to a body whose conduct meets the criteria specified in s.43 of the 2014 Act.

7.28   While there is the possibility of conflict between the ASB provisions of the 2014 Act and the statutory nuisance provisions of the EPA 1990, the legal tests applying to the two regimes are different. The threshold for statutory nuisance is a high one. Under the nuisance limb of statutory nuisance, material and substantial interference with personal comfort is the test. Mere annoyance would fall below the threshold for nuisance but would be enough in a case of ASB, provided that all the ingredients of s.43 were made out.

7.29   The range of behaviours that could be anti-social is not limited in the 2014 Act; it even includes allowing an invasion of Japanese Knotweed onto neighbouring land.[32] By contrast, statutory nuisances are limited to the list provided in s.79(1) of the EPA 1990. Some forms of statutory nuisance only apply to industrial, trade, and business premises. For example, cooking smells from domestic premises could not be a statutory nuisance but could amount to ASB under the 2014 Act.

7.30   Where an investigation is being carried out under the EPA 1990, it would usually be inadvisable to issue a CPN. However, it may be appropriate to issue a CPN, for example if:

- an investigation is taking a long time to establish whether or not a statutory nuisance exists;
- in a statutory noise nuisance case, where the local authority believes an alternative to serving an abatement notice is likely to be effective;[33]
- where the investigation concludes that a statutory nuisance is not made out.

Closure Notices and Closure Orders

7.31   Authorised council and police officers have the power to close premises, including residential premises, that are causing a nuisance or are associated with disorder. The powers are set down in sections 76–93 of the Anti-social Behaviour, Crime and Policing Act 2014 and explained further in the Home Office Guidance.[34] The Closure Notice can be used without the need to go to court and is limited in duration to twenty-four hours, with the possibility of extending it to a maximum of forty-eight hours. Following the issuing of a Closure

Notice, an application must be made to the magistrates' court for a Closure Order in order to extend the terms to a maximum of six months. If an application for a court order is not made, the Closure Notice comes to an end.

7.32 The test for issuing a Closure Notice is where the local authority or police are satisfied on reasonable grounds that:

- the use of particular premises has resulted, or (if the notice is not issued) is likely soon to result, in nuisance to members of the public; or
- there has been, or (if the notice is not issued) is likely soon to be, disorder near those premises associated with the use of those premises; and
- the notice is necessary to prevent the nuisance or disorder from continuing, recurring, or occurring.

7.33 The use of a Closure Notice is draconian, particularly in relation to residential property. The Home Office Guidance suggests that it could be used to deal with illegal raves or noisy parties where large numbers of people are present. A Closure Notice cannot prohibit access to an owner or person normally resident at the premises. However, a Closure Order, granted by the court, can prohibit access to those who routinely live at the premises.

Injunctions

7.34 Injunctive relief is the remedy most frequently sought in a private nuisance case, where proceedings can be brought in the High Court or in the county courts. Injunctions are a civil remedy granted at the discretion of the court; there is no requirement to add a claim for damages when seeking an injunction.

7.35 Injunctions also feature in civil proceedings in public nuisance. A local authority is able to seek an injunction in its own name in respect of a public nuisance in order to protect the interests of the public.[35] Making the decision to seek an injunction is no different in principle from any other council decision, and it may be delegated to a subcommittee or officer with sufficient authority.

7.36 A local authority may also apply for an injunction to the High Court, under s.81(5) of the EPA 1990 "for the purpose of securing the abatement, prohibition or restriction" of any statutory nuisance. Care is needed in a statutory nuisance case to ensure that an injunction is being sought on proper grounds. Clear reasons why proceedings using the abatement notice procedure would afford an inadequate remedy need to be given to the High Court. The inconvenience of the abatement notice procedure would not constitute sufficient grounds for making an application. In *Vale of White Horse*, the statutory nuisance was believed to result from excessive smells and effluvia emanating from an expanding pig farm business.[36] The application for an injunction by the local authority failed, Bell J finding that it would be necessary to show that the defendant has been "deliberately or flagrantly flouting the law" and that only an injunction is going to stop the activity causing the nuisance.[37]

7.37 A history of non-compliance with abatement notices may not be enough to obtain an injunction. In the statutory nuisance injunction case of *The Barns (NE) Ltd & Suleman v Newcastle City Council*, Sir Christopher Staughton opined:

> *It will not always be the case that the service of an abatement notice would be futile, even if the wrongdoer was shown to have been reluctant to comply with the law in the past. It may be that an abatement notice on a later occasion would procure compliance from the wrongdoer. It cannot be assumed that he is going to disregard the notice as he had done in the past. The aim, after all, of this part of the law is to persuade people not to infringe against it, rather than to promote the enforcement of the law.[38]*

Application for an injunction under the Anti-social Behaviour, Crime and Policing Act 2014

7.38 Applications for an injunction should be made either to the county court or to the High Court. Applications in respect of individuals aged from ten to eighteen should be made to the youth court. Unlike the limitations previously discussed for seeking an injunction, civil injunctions to control ASB are intended to be used as a **primary** remedy under Part 1 of the Anti-social Behaviour, Crime and Policing Act 2014. In other words, an injunction sought under this statute should not be seen as a remedy of last resort. Injunctions – alongside the other measures laid down in the Act – are at the forefront of powers to control ASB. This primary role for the ASB injunction applies to all the agencies having powers to apply for it under Part 1 of the 2014 Act. The Statutory Guidance issued by the government also states that injunctions should be considered early on in appropriate cases:

> *[An injunction] can offer fast and effective protection for victims and communities and set a clear standard of behaviour for perpetrators, stopping the person's behaviour from escalating.[39]*

7.39   The grounds for seeking an injunction must be fairly and properly made out, however, as this is a draconian remedy. The tests are not the same for ASB injunctions as for CPNs. As provided in s.2(1)(a) of the 2014 Act, the test for an ASB injunction in a "non-housing related" context is "conduct that has caused, or is likely to cause, harassment, alarm or distress to any person". This sets quite a high threshold of harm; it applies to more serious forms of ASB, close to what would be required for a criminal offence. It is applicable where there is a relatively serious ASB problem in a public place, such as a town or city centre, shopping mall, or local park.

7.40   For ASB in a housing context, the "nuisance or annoyance" test will apply, and this sets a lower threshold compared to ASB in a public place. The test for an injunction in a housing context is where the conduct "is capable of causing nuisance or annoyance to a person in relation to that person's occupation of residential premises".[40] This test applies not just to occupiers of residential premises but also to any person affected by the "'housing-related' nuisance or annoyance.[41] In a housing context, therefore, it is permissible to seek an injunction to control behaviour falling below the nuisance threshold. This will be appropriate if there are reasonable grounds to believe that the behaviour is likely to worsen over time unless checked by an injunction.

7.41   Social landlords, as well as local authorities and the police, are able to apply for an injunction in respect of the "housing-related" provisions, where it concerns a person's occupation of residential premises. Care must be taken to ensure that the grounds for seeking an injunction in this situation are properly made out. In cases where the terms of the injunction are breached, the grounds for evicting the offending tenant will be made out. Unless the case is very serious, consideration should be given to whether issuing a CPN might be more proportionate than seeking an injunction.

Notes

1 See DTLR, *Housing Disrepair Housing Disrepair Legal Obligations: Good Practice Guidance* (2002). Available at: https://assets.publishing.service.gov.uk/government/uploads/system/uploads/attachment_data/file/7852/142949.pdf
2 See, for example: *Nottingham City District Council v Newton* [1974] 1 WLR 923 and *Salford City Council v McNally* [1976] AC 379.
3 See Chapter 4.
4 [1999] 31 HLR 545.
5 EPA 1990, s.160.
6 [1999] 2 All ER 609.
7 *Ibid.*
8 *Watkins v Aged Merchant Seamen's Homes & Another* [2018] EWHC 2410 (Admin).

9   See, for example, Appendix C in Luba J, Foster D, and Prevatt B, *Repairs: Tenants Rights*, 5th edition (London: LAG, 2016).
10 Criminal Procedure Rules 2015 (SI 2015/1490).
11 EPA 1990, s.82(2).
12 *R (on the application of Knowsley MBC) v Williams* [2001] Env LR 28.
13 *Birmingham City DC v McMahon* [1987] 19 HLR 452.
14 Nominally Level 5 as set by the Criminal Justice Act 1982, but since 2014 there is no limit. Guidelines for environmental offences can be found in *Environmental Offences: Definitive Guideline*, Sentencing Council, 2014 (sentencingcouncil.org.uk).
15 *R v Dudley Magistrates' Court, ex p Hollis and anor* [1998] Env LR 354.
16 May 1997, *Legal Action* 21.
17 *Warner v London Borough of Lambeth* [1984] 15 HLR 42, DC.
18 [1995] 28 HLR 747, DC.
19 See also: *Carr v Hackney LBC* [1995] 28 HLR 747; *Adeniregun v Southwark LBC* [1996], *Legal Action* 21, May 1997; *Jones v Walsall MBC* [2002] EWHC 1232 (Admin).
20 *Legal Action*, December 2013.
21 The tenant had argued for a damages award calculated on the principles of *English Churches Housing Group v Shine* [2004] EWCA Civ 434, where damages were claimed against the landlord for breaches of the repairing covenants implied by s.11 of the Landlord and Tenant Act 1985, but the judge rejected this.
22 *R v Liverpool Crown Court and Liverpool City Council, ex part Cooke* [1996] 4 All ER 589.
23 *Legal Action*, May 1997.
24 Carr H, Cowan D, Kirton-Darling E, and Burtonshaw-Gunn E, *Closing the Gaps: Health and Safety at Home* (2017). Available at: https://england.shelter.org.uk/__data/assets/pdf_file/0010/1457551/2017_11_14_Closing_the_Gaps_-_Health_and_Safety_at_Home.pdf
25 See Chapter 4.
26 See, for example, Rugg J and Rhodes D, *The Evolving Private Rented Sector: Its Contribution and Potential* (University of York, Centre for Housing Policy, 2018). Available at: www.york.ac.uk/media/news-and-events/pressreleases/2018/the-evolving-private-rented-sector.pdf
27 *Anti-social Behaviour, Crime and Policing Act 2014, Reform of Anti-social Behaviour Powers: Statutory Guidance for Frontline Professionals* (HM Government: Home Office, December 2017).
28 *Professional Practice Note: Revised Guidance on the Use of Community Protection Notices under Part 4 of the Anti-social Behaviour, Crime and Policing Act 2014* (London: CIEH, November 2017).
29 Pursuant to s.53 of the 2014 Act, the Secretary of State has ordered that "housing providers" (broadly, Registered Social Landlords) be designated as "other persons" by the relevant local authority to serve CPNs and related Fixed Penalty Notices (FPNs).
30 Housing and Planning Act 2016 (Banning Order Offences) Regulations 2018 (2018/216), Schedule Offences.
31 Housing and Planning Act 2016, s.14(1).
32 *Reform of Anti-social Behaviour Powers: Japanese Knotweed and Other Invasive Non-native Plants* (HM Government: Home Office, 2014).

33 The local authority has a period of seven days to delay serving an abatement notice in these circumstances, as provided by s.80(2A)–(2C) EPA 1990.

34 *Anti-social Behaviour, Crime and Policing Act 2014, Reform of Anti-social Behaviour Powers: Statutory Guidance for Frontline Professionals* (HM Government: Home Office, December 2017).

35 Local Government Act 1972, s.222, provides this power in civil proceedings in public nuisance where "a local authority consider it expedient for the promotion or protection of the interests of the inhabitants of their area".

36 *Vale of White Horse DC v Allen & Partners* [1997] Env LR 212.

37 *Ibid.*, 212, 214.

38 [2005] EWCA Civ 1274, para 15.

39 *Reform of Anti-social Behaviour Powers: Statutory Guidance for Frontline Professionals* (HM Government: Home Office, December 2017), p. 21.

40 Anti-social Behaviour, Crime and Policing Act 2014, s.2(1)(b).

41 *Ibid.*, s.2(1)(c).

8 Resolving problems with residential property

Introduction

8.01 We have seen that local authorities are placed under a duty to keep housing conditions under review and have considered the circumstances when an inspection should be carried out utilising Part 1 of the Housing Act 2004. Part III of the Environmental Protection Act 1990 in relation to statutory nuisances is also important and should be used in certain, more limited situations. In both cases, when an inspection is undertaken, it is the whole dwelling that has to be inspected. This enables all the deficiencies that contribute to a hazard to be identified and for the risks of exposure to any hazard to be properly assessed. In regard to statutory nuisance, it is the premises as a whole that need to be assessed in order to decide whether they are in such a state as to be prejudicial to health or a nuisance. Either one major defect or multiple defects that individually might seem minor but together become problematic make the premises prejudicial to health.

8.02 It should be clear to practitioners that the courts have interpreted the meaning of "health" more narrowly in the statutory nuisance provisions of the EPA 1990 than in the Housing Act 2004 and the HHSRS. With the latter regime, health is defined in terms of an individual's state of physical, mental, and social wellbeing. It is not limited to the presence or absence of disease, infirmity, or physical injury but includes psychological injuries and distress.

8.03 The main form of statutory nuisance we have been concerned with in this monograph is s.79(1)(a) of the EPA 1990: the state of residential premises. For the statutory nuisance regime to be available, the premises have to have "fallen" into a state of disrepair, amounting to a nuisance at common law or a risk of injury to health. Deficiencies in design cannot be remedied under the statutory nuisance regime. No such limitation applies to the HHSRS where design deficiencies are often responsible for hazards. Inadequate ventilation (leading to carbon monoxide or excess heat hazards) and even the building materials used (e.g. asbestos and human-made mineral fibres) could contribute to a hazard.

8.04 In this chapter, we look at some of the differences and similarities between the statutory nuisance and the Housing Act 2004 regimes. We consider practice and procedural issues, as well as some of the limitations of both provisions. Alternatives for addressing problems in and around residential premises will also be discussed.

Matters that cannot be dealt with under the Environmental Protection Act 1990

Noise (other than noise emitted from premises)

8.05 It is now well established that noise problems that are attributable to the structure of the building – rather than because of neighbours being noisy – cannot be dealt with under the statutory nuisance provisions. The premises are not in such a state as to be a nuisance at common law[1] or prejudicial to health.[2] So, where the EHP comes across such problems, the only route would be to use Part 1 of the Housing Act 2004 where the deficiencies giving rise to the hazard can be identified.

Accidents and physical injury

8.06 When using the HHSRS, the fact that the building complied with the Building Regulations and Approved Documents applicable at the time of construction is not a relevant consideration. It can be the case that elements of construction that comply with the Building Regulations can still give rise to a hazard. For example, "paddle" or "alternate tread" space-saver stairs might be permissible under the Building Regulations but could still be assessed as hazardous given that the vulnerable age group for "falling on stairs" etc., against whom the stairs should be assessed, consists of those people aged sixty years and over. However, the hazard score does not dictate the course of action to take under the Housing Act 2004, even if it is assessed as a Category 1 hazard.

8.07 Defects that could lead to accidents or unintentional injuries do not come within the scope of the statutory nuisance regime. So, for example, poorly designed stairs[3] or amenities that cannot be reached safely (such as an openable window) would be outside the scope of statutory nuisance. Where there is any risk of physical injury, the route to a remedy would lie either with dangerous structures legislation (s.77 Building Act 1984) or the Housing Act 2004 – including use of the HHSRS (which includes the various "falling" hazards, as well as such hazards as "Position and Operability of Amenities" and "Structural Collapse and Falling Elements").

8.08   There is some question whether dangerous electrical installations could fall within the scope of statutory nuisance. In a non-binding decision in the Crown Court, it was decided that dangerous electrical wiring could lead to a fire, and, as fire and the smoke produced would be injurious to health, it was decided that the premises were in such a state as to be prejudicial to health.[4] This decision is not binding, however, and is arguably wrong because it impermissibly extends the scope of the state of premises in s.79(1)(a) EPA 1990.

Problems that may be addressed in different ways

Tents, caravans, sheds, and other accommodation

8.09   In the Housing Act 2004, reference is made to "residential premises", which *inter alia* means a "dwelling", defined as "a building or part of a building occupied or intended to be occupied as a separate dwelling".[5] The issue is whether a structure like a shed, garage or mobile home comes within the definition of a "building" in the Act; if it does, then the powers provided by the Act may become available. In a case in Darlington, the First-tier Tribunal held that a caravan that was occupied as a dwelling did not come within the definition of a building.[6] The Tribunal considered an earlier Tribunal decision, which had found that a caravan – occupied in conjunction with an adjoining, conventionally built building – did come within the definition of a building.[7] The issue in the Darlington case was over whether the caravan, as a separate entity not linked to another structure on the land, was intended for use as a residential dwelling. In the Darlington case, the caravan was found to be a structure that was not intended to be used as a dwelling, and hence it fell outside the scope of the Housing Act 2004.

8.10   For unconventional premises used as dwellings, it is possible to act where they are considered to contain Category 1 hazards and are unsuitable to be used as accommodation. A few years ago, the London Borough of Hounslow made a Demolition Order on an outbuilding let as a separate dwelling in the garden of a property. The property was being used for residential purposes but lacked any basic amenities and was built partly on a boundary wall. The order was appealed, and the First-tier Tribunal confirmed the order.[8] The London Borough of Hillingdon have also made Demolition Orders under s.265 of the Housing Act 1985 (as amended by the Housing Act 2004) on outbuildings, including garden sheds that were rented out as accommodation. Although beyond the scope of this publication, some local authorities have utilised planning legislation to address the problem of "beds in sheds".[9]

8.11   If it is not possible to use Housing Act powers, then there remains s.268 of the Public Health Act 1936. This provision is included as a statutory nuisance by s.79(1)(h) EPA 1990. Section 268 of the 1936 Act controls the use of temporary and other unsuitable structures for housing. Section 268 applies to a tent, van, shed, or similar structure used for human habitation:

> a   *which is in such a state, or so overcrowded, as to be prejudicial to the health of the inmates; or*
>
> b   *the use of which, by reason of the absence of proper sanitary accommodation or otherwise, gives rise, whether on the site or on other land, to a nuisance or to conditions prejudicial to health.*

8.12   Where a local authority is satisfied that a statutory nuisance has resulted under s.268 of the 1936 Act, an abatement notice should be served on the occupier.[10] The "occupier" includes any person for the time being in charge of that accommodation.[11] It is a defence for the person served with a notice to prove that he or she did not authorise the tent, van, shed, or other structure to be stationed or erected on the land.[12]

8.13   Where a prosecution is successful, the powers of the court include making an order prohibiting the use for human habitation of the tent, van, shed, or other structure in question at such places or within such area as may be specified.[13]

Drainage problems

8.14   A range of provisions can be used to deal with drainage problems. That said, many drains and sewers are these days the responsibility of the water and sewerage companies (WASCs). It is perhaps useful to define what a drain is and what a sewer is. It has generally been regarded that a sewer is a pipe that serves more than one premises, whereas a drain serves only one premises or building. Section 219(1) of the Water Industry Act 1991 provides that a "drain" means "a drain used for the drainage of one building or of any buildings or yards appurtenant to buildings within the same curtilage". Any other pipeline would be a sewer. The Court of Appeal has held that a pipe constructed as a sewer remains a sewer and not a drain, even where it receives effluent from only one property.[14]

8.15   The issue used to be whether a "sewer" was a private sewer or a "public sewer" (vested in the sewerage undertaker). Since 1 October 2011, this should no longer have been an issue, as all gravity sewers and lateral drains that drain into the public sewerage system have been adopted by the WASCs as part of the public sewerage system. The effect of this is that a drain from a building becomes a "public lateral" once it passes beyond the "curtilage". In law, there are no longer any "private sewers".

8.16   Section 59 of the Building Act 1984 (as amended)[15] provides local authorities with the power to require an owner of a building (as defined by s.126 of the 1984 Act) to remedy a drain or similar apparatus. Section 59 provides:

1   If it appears to a local authority that in the case of a building –

a   satisfactory provision has not been, and ought to be, made for drainage . . .,

b   a cesspool, private sewer, drain, soil pipe, rain-water pipe, spout, sink or other necessary appliance provided for the building is insufficient or, in the case of a private sewer or drain communicating directly or indirectly with a public sewer, is so defective as to admit subsoil water,

c   a cesspool or other such work or appliance as aforesaid provided for the building is in such a condition as to be prejudicial to health or a nuisance, or

d   a cesspool, private sewer or drain formerly used for the drainage of the building, but no longer used for it, is prejudicial to health or a nuisance,

they shall by notice require the owner of the building to make satisfactory provision for the drainage of the building, or, as the case may be, require either the owner or the occupier of the building to do such work as may be necessary for renewing, repairing or cleansing the existing cesspool, sewer, drain, pipe, spout, sink or other appliance, or for filling up, removing or otherwise rendering innocuous the disused cesspool, sewer or drain.

This is a useful provision that should not be overlooked. It provides a way for local authorities to deal with "misconnections" resulting in the pollution of water courses. This can occur when drains that should conduct only surface water are used to take grey or foul water, such as from washing machines.

8.17 Section 60 of the Building Act 1984 is concerned with the use and ventilation of soil pipes; it provides:

> *1 A pipe for conveying rain-water from a roof shall not be used for the purpose of conveying the soil or drainage from a sanitary convenience.*
>
> *2 The soil pipe from a water-closet shall be properly ventilated.*
>
> *3 A pipe for conveying surface water from premises shall not be permitted to act as a ventilating shaft to a drain or sewer conveying foul water.*
>
> *4 If it appears to the local authority . . . that there is on any premises a contravention of any provision of this section, they may by notice require the owner or the occupier of those premises to execute such work as may be necessary to remedy the matter.*

8.18 Only the owner of the premises can be served under s.59 of the Building Act 1984 to make proper provision, but under s.60 either the owner or the occupier may be required to take the action required. Under s.98 of the Act:

> *If, on a complaint made by the owner of premises, it appears to a magistrates' court that the occupier of those premises prevents the owner from executing any work that he is by or under this Act required to execute, the court may order the occupier to permit the execution of the work.*

8.19 Local authorities have powers to repair drains etc. and to remedy stopped-up drains under s.17 of the Public Health Act 1961, which provides:

> *1 If it appears to a local authority that a drain, private sewer, water-closet, waste pipe or soil pipe –*
>
> > *a is not sufficiently maintained and kept in good repair, and*
> > *b can be sufficiently repaired at a cost not exceeding £250,*
>
> *the local authority may, after giving not less than seven days notice to the person or persons concerned, cause the drain, private sewer, water-closet or pipe to be repaired and . . . recover the expenses reasonably incurred in so doing, so far as they do not exceed £250, from the person or persons concerned, in such proportions, if there is more than one such person, as the local authority may determine.*

Given the cost limit, this provision might not be very helpful as an alternative to using s.59 of the Building Act 1984.

8.20   It may seem strange that so many provisions of the old Public Health Acts remain in force and thus able to provide a remedy in certain situations. For example, under s.45(1) of the Public Health Act 1936:

> *If it appears to a local authority that any closets provided for or in connection with a building are in such a state as to be prejudicial to health or a nuisance, but that they can without reconstruction be put into a satisfactory condition, the authority shall by notice require the owner or the occupier of the building to execute such works, or to take such steps by cleansing the closets or otherwise, as may be necessary for that purpose.*

The same provisions for appeals and for the conduct of proceedings generally apply as for any other type of statutory nuisance in Part III of the EPA 1990.

8.21   Another venerable power is provided by s.22 of the 1961 Public Health Act:

> *A local authority may, on the application of the owner or occupier of any premises, undertake the cleansing or repair of any drains, water-closets, sinks or gullies in or connected with the premises, and may recover from the applicant such reasonable charge, if any, for so doing as they think fit.*

Given that most local authorities no longer have "drain teams", this provision is probably redundant these days.

8.22   In many cases where there is a drainage defect, including a blockage, the premises affected could be considered to be in such as state as to be prejudicial to health, under s.79 of the EPA 1990. In *Bradford MDC v Yorkshire Water Services Ltd*,[16] both parties accepted that, where a pipeline discharged sewage over the garden of a house not actually served by that pipe, the premises were in such a state as to be a statutory nuisance. At issue was whether or not the pipeline was a public sewer. It was decided that it was not a public sewer and that therefore Yorkshire Water was not the person responsible for causing the statutory nuisance. Action can be taken against the WASC, however, when sewage escapes from a blocked public sewer (or public lateral drain) and causes any premises affected to be in such as state as to be prejudicial to health.

8.23   This case should be compared with *East Riding of Yorkshire Council v Yorkshire Water Services Ltd*,[17] where it was held that a blocked public sewer was not "premises in such as state as to be prejudicial to health or a nuisance". This might seem strange but sewerage law is complex and old. This case hinged on a Victorian case, which held that a public sewer could not be "premises" in the context of (what is now) s.79(1)(a) of the EPA 1990.[18]

8.24 In *Hounslow London Borough Council v Thames Water Utilities Ltd*,[19] the problem was due to smells affecting residential premises close to a sewage treatment works. In July 2001, Hounslow LBC served an abatement notice on Thames Water under s.80(1) of the EPA 1990. The notice specified that an odour amounting to a nuisance had occurred and was likely to recur at premises known as Mogden Sewage Treatment Works, for which the company was responsible. The company appealed against the notice to the magistrates' court. A preliminary hearing was held to determine whether the sewage works constituted "premises" within the context of s.79(1)(d) of the 1990 Act, i.e. statutory nuisances arising from "smells or other effluvia". The district judge quashed the notice. He was of the opinion that sewage works were excluded from the operation of s 79(1)(d) and relied on *Parlby*, which had held that "premises" were not apt to embrace sewage works.[20]

8.25 The local authority then appealed to the Divisional Court, which decided that sewage works were not excluded from the operation of s.79(1)(d) of the EPA 1990. It was held that it was necessary to distinguish between s.79(1)(a) EPA 1990 – which concerns statutory nuisances arising from the state of the premises – from those arising from smells and other effluvia: s.79(1)(d) of the Act. The Divisional Court decided that, although the *Parlby* construction of the word "premises" was still applicable to s.79(1)(a), it was not permissible to transplant that construction to s.79(1)(d).

8.26 Problems with drainage are also capable of being addressed by Part 1 of the Housing Act 2004. Two HHSRS hazards may be relevant the first is Personal Hygiene, Sanitation and Drainage. This cover threats of infection and threats to mental health associated with personal hygiene, including from facilities for personal washing and the washing of clothes, sanitation, and drainage. Problems with pests associated with defective drainage facilities are not included.

8.27 This type of hazard can also be caused by inadequate ventilation to a soil or waste pipe, disrepair and defects to the foul or waste water drainage systems, and defects to a soil or waste pipe serving a water-using facility. Where there is a private sewerage system, such as a septic tank, the HHSRS can take account of defects to that system. Surface water drainage is also something to be considered, so that a missing, defective or badly located soakaway for surface water can contribute to the hazard. The lack of an adequately sized soil or waste pipe connected to a water-using facility, able to carry foul or waste water safely to the drainage system, is also a matter relevant to the hazard.

8.28   The other relevant hazard (also a consideration when there is a pest problem) is Domestic Hygiene Pests and Refuse. This can take account of disrepair to drains – including sewers and/or inspection chambers – that permit rodents to escape and enter the property.

8.29   Finally on drainage (although this might be better considered as external or land drainage) is the matter of ditches, which, if not maintained, can lead to flooding that affects residential premises. Section 259(1)(a) of the Public Health Act 1936 defines as a statutory nuisance "any pond, pool, ditch, gutter or watercourse which is so foul or in such a state as to be prejudicial to health or a nuisance". Section 259(1)(b) of the Act is concerned with obstruction of non-navigable watercourses.

Pests and vermin

8.30   The Public Health Act 1936, s.83, provides a power for a local authority to require an owner or occupier to take steps to cleanse and disinfect filthy or verminous premises. The local authority may carry out requirements in default and recover expenses and/or prosecute.

8.31   The Prevention of Damage by Pests Act 1949, s.4 is also available for local authorities to address problems resulting from rats and mice. If it is considered that steps should be taken for the destruction of rats or mice on the land or to keep the land free of them, the local authority may serve a notice on the owner or occupier of the land. The notice can require him to take steps to destroy the rodents or to keep the land free of them within a reasonable period, as specified. Where the owner of the land is not also the occupier, separate notices should be served on both. Any appeals against the notice are to the magistrates' court. Should there be a failure to comply with a notice, the local authority has the power to carry out the steps specified and recover expenses incurred.

8.32   It is now quite clear that premises that are infested with vermin (including cockroaches, rats, and mice) could be considered prejudicial to health and therefore a statutory nuisance, under s.79(1)(a) of the EPA 1990.[21] Sometimes mice have been considered only as a "nuisance pest", but there is increasing evidence that they also provide a reservoir of infection and can cause ill-health in humans.[22]

Where defects allow rodents to enter the property, the hygiene (and pest proofing) of premises is a consideration for abating the statutory nuisance. The steps or works that are needed to achieve this can be specified in the abatement notice served on the owner of the property.

8.33 Alternatively, as we have seen, the HHSRS and Part 1 of the 2004 Act is available to address this problem. Domestic Hygiene Pests & Refuse pertains to matters that are the responsibility of the owner, such as disrepair enabling pests to enter or escape from the drainage system. For this hazard to be applicable, there have to be deficiencies that compromise domestic hygiene and permit pests to enter the residential premises, including yards and garden. The mere presence of pests will not necessarily be capable of being remedied using the HHSRS; the infestation must be shown to result from deficiencies in the premises.

Which regulatory approach to take?

8.34 We have seen that many powers available to local authorities, other than those in the Housing Act 2004, are derived from the statutory nuisance provisions in the Environmental Protection Act 1990. So, faced with a problem in or around residential premises, will the Housing Act 2004 or the EPA 1990 provide the more appropriate remedy? Are any procedural differences provided by these separate legislative regimes that might influence the decision? Some similarities as well as differences might influence which route to take when dealing with a public health problem associated with residential premises. For some less extensive problems, the statutory nuisance regime might provide a more proportionate approach, assuming that the deficiencies fall within the scope of Part III EPA 1990.

8.35 **Table 8.1** summarises some of the differences and similarities between the provisions in the EPA 1990 and the Housing Act 2004. To recap some of the things to bear in mind: The threshold for a nuisance is generally not as high under the statutory nuisance regime compared to when something is alleged to be prejudicial to health. A fundamental requirement for the nuisance limb to apply is for the problem to have originated on neighbouring premises and to cause harm to those in the affected premises. For example, a blocked gutter causing the gutter to overflow when it rains will not make the premises a nuisance if the only impact is dampness in the bedroom of that same property (though it could be argued to be prejudicial to health). If, however, it causes dampness in the bedroom of the adjoining property, it could be argued that the premises are in such a state as to be a nuisance.

8.36   The Housing Act 2004, on the other hand, is not concerned with nearby property or land but focuses exclusively on the residential premises forming the subject of regulatory action. Any assessment of these residential premises includes any:

> *paths, yards, gardens, and outbuildings etc that are associated or for use with, or give access to that dwelling, whether or not they are for the exclusive use of that dwelling, or are shared with other dwellings and any rights of way, easements, and common or shared parts and services necessary for the occupation and use of the dwelling, for example non-adopted footpaths, drives, and drains.*[23]

8.37   Which of the two main provisions covered in this monograph to use as the basis for an intervention will be a matter of professional judgement. There will instances when it might be obvious which provides the more appropriate route but also times when they represent genuine options. The statutory nuisance provisions might be useful where there is one obvious defect causing the premises to be prejudicial to health or a nuisance. Statutory nuisance will be exclusively relevant when the defect is causing a nuisance or risk to health affecting a neighbouring property. Matters that involve a risk of physical injury will, however, be outside the scope of statutory nuisance.

8.38   Where there are a number of deficiencies – particularly if some are the result of poor design rather than dilapidation – then Part 1 of the Housing Act 2004 is likely to be the more appropriate route. Indeed, if the problems identified are not ones resulting from the property falling into a dilapidated state, then s.79(1)(a) of the EPA 1990 will not be appropriate and only the Housing Act provisions will be available.

8.39   In all situations where local authorities are acting as regulators, a fair and proportionate approach to enforcement is required. So where the problems in premises are relatively minor (but there are still risks), it might be more appropriate to use the Hazard Awareness Notice rather than take more intrusive action under the Housing Act 2004.

8.40   While great care should be taken not to confuse the requirements of the EPA 1990 and the Housing Act 2004, the Operating Guidance for the HHSRS can generally be used as guidance to justify why premises are thought to be prejudicial to health. For example, where there are only drainage problems, it might be more appropriate to use the Building Act 1984 or the statutory nuisance provisions. In these circumstances, the HHSRS Guidance can still be used to justify an opinion that a state of affairs poses a risk to health.

Table 8.1 Checklist of Environmental Protection Act and Housing Act provisions

Environmental Protection Act 1990	Housing Act 2004
• Schedule 3 of 1990 Act – authorised person may enter at any reasonable time, but for residential premises, except in emergency, shall give occupier 24 hours' notice.	• 24 hours' notice of intention to inspect, is given to owner (if known) and occupier (if any) – s.239.
• After investigation and only if satisfied that a statutory nuisance exists, shall serve an abatement notice; no explanation required for how the decision of statutory nuisance arrived at.	• Duty to take one of the courses of action. If Category 1 hazard, discretion to take one of the available forms of action. For Category 2 hazards, there are options for action and Hazard Rating is just the first step.
• Abatement notice (the only course of action under the 1990 Act, save an injunction) served on person responsible; where nuisance arises from any defect of a structural character, served on owner of the premises.	• Service of Improvement Notice etc. on person having control; or in the case of HMO the licence holder, if licensed, otherwise the manager or person having control etc. (schedule 1). Alternative courses of action available, such as suspended Improvement Notice, Prohibition Order (which can be suspended), or Hazard Awareness Notice. LA has to show why action is "most appropriate" with Statement of Reasons.
• No *pro-forma* notice in 1990 Act.	
• Abatement notice can be a "simple" notice, although this is not good practice where there are obvious defects of a structural nature with a property.	
• Appeal to the magistrates' court within 21 days of service.	• Where imminent risk of serious harm, then Emergency Remedial Action or Emergency Prohibition Order is available.
• Offence: failure to comply with notice without reasonable excuse.	• Content of notices and order specified in the Act.
• Where non-compliance with notice, LA may do whatever is necessary to execute notice.	• Appeal to the First-tier Tribunal (Property Chamber) (Residential), within 21 days for Improvement Notice and 28 days for Prohibition Order. In Wales, appeal to Residential Property Tribunal.
• Notice can be withdrawn.	• Offence – failing to comply with Improvement Notice or contravention of Prohibition Order without reasonable excuse. No offence of not complying with Hazard Awareness Notice.
	• If not complied with, power to undertake works with Improvement Notice, with or without agreement.
	• Notice cannot be withdrawn; if found to be incorrect, has to be revoked.
	• Notice can be varied, e.g. if alternative works proposed will address the hazard.

Notes

1 *Southwark LBC v Mills, Tanner; Baxter v Camden London Borough Council*[2001] 1 AC 1.
2 *R (on the application of Vella) v Lambeth London Borough Council* [2005] EWHC 2473 (Admin).
3 *R (on the application of) v Bristol City Council ex parte Everett* [1999] EWCA Civ 869.
4 *Bennett v Preston Borough Council* [1982] April 1983 *Environmental Health.*
5 Housing Act 2004, s.99. This definition applies to Part 3 of the Act: the licensing of non-HMO residential housing.
6 Darlington BC. Caravans to the rear of 20 and 50 Clifton Road, Darlington DL1 5DS MAN/00EH/HPO/2013/0002 & 0003.
7 Arun DC and St Edmunds Cottage, Houghton Sussex in June 2008 CHI/45UC/HIN/2008/0005.
8 LON/ooAT/HDO/2013/0002 – Second Rear Dwelling (Timber 3), 33 Station Road, TW3 2AP.
9 It has been reported that Ealing LBC secured fines totalling £450,000 for breaches of planning law by a landlord who illegally converted sheds and a garage for living accommodation and failed to comply with enforcement notices. Available at: https://ealingnewsextra.co.uk/latest-news/huge-fine-for-beds-in-sheds-southall-landlord and www.ealing.gov.uk/news/article/1841/huge_fine_for_beds_in_sheds_southall_landlord. Ealing LBC had secured another conviction of a landlord for a similar offence a few weeks previously.
10 Public Health Act 1936, s.268(3).
11 Public Health Act 1936, s.268(2).
12 *Ibid.*, s.268(3).
13 *Ibid.*, s.268(5).
14 *Bromley LBC v Morritt* [2000] EHLR 24.
15 Amended by the Building (Amendment) Regulations 2001 (SI 2001/3335), reg.3(4)(a).
16 [2002] 10 EG 159.
17 [2001] Env LR 113.
18 *R v Parlby* [1889] 22 QBD 520.
19 [2003] EWHC 1197 (Admin).
20 *R v Parlby* [1889] 22 QBD 520.
21 *Birmingham City Council v Oakley* [2001] 1 All ER 385,392.
22 Bonnefoy X, Kampen H, and Sweeney K, *Public Health Significance of Urban Pests*, (Copenhagen, Denmark: WHO Europe, 2008).
23 Housing Act 2004, s.1(5)(6).

9 Case studies

This chapter is about the practical application of much that has been covered in the previous chapters. In these case studies, some initial information is provided; and then readers are asked to consider some questions on the basis that gaps are left in the information provided which readers might wish to think about. Later in each case study, you will find some further information and possible responses suggested.

CASE STUDY 1

9.01   The property – 101a Chadwick Street – is a ground floor self-contained flat in an end of terrace property, constructed approximately 100 years ago. It is a corner property with the flank wall on Duncan Street. At some time, twenty to thirty years ago, it was converted from a corner shop with flat into two self-contained flats. The elderly woman tenant, who has lived there for about nine months, has complained about dampness in the property since October (it is now December). The owner of the flat is a registered housing provider (housing association), who has dismissed complaints as the tenant's fault. The building is of solid wall construction, partially rendered externally, and is entered directly off the street. Stairs in the common hallway lead to the upper flat. The flat which is the subject of the complaint is entered from the common entrance hall (there is no other route of access or exit). The flat itself has a small hallway from which the bedroom, bathroom, and living room are entered. The kitchen is entered directly from the living room. The flat has a mixture of solid and suspended timber floors. The internal combined WC/bathroom has mechanical ventilation, operated by the light switch. A wall partially separates the part of the room containing the bath from that containing the WC and wash-hand basin. The landlord has provided a retractable washing line over the bath. The windows to the bedroom and kitchen are uPVC double-glazed with trickle vents. The two windows to the living room are timber double hung, sliding sash, single glazed (one faces on to Chadwick Street, the other on to Duncan Street). Space heating is by central heating with radiators in the living room, bathroom, and bedroom; the wall-mounted gas-fired boiler, which also provides the hot water supply, is in the kitchen.

Inspection findings

1   Areas of damp and mould affected wall plaster in the kitchen (two areas of approximately 0.5 square metre): one behind the refrigerator and adjacent to an air brick in the wall, and another at a higher level below the extractor fan in the wall, adjacent to the party wall with the adjoining property.

2   There is a step down into the kitchen (solid floor) of approximately 100 millimetre and a similar step down into the part of the bathroom containing the bath.

3   The door to the kitchen is ill-fitting and cannot be closed shut.

4   Areas (3 square metres approximately in total) of damp and mould affected wall plaster to the two external walls of the living room situated in the corner of the building (this room has a suspended timber floor covered with carpet).

5   Ill-fitting and draughty sash windows to the living room (one is difficult to open).

6   Area of perished wall plaster to the flank wall of living room (1.5 metres approximately).

7   Fresh mouse droppings found in the kitchen cupboards and also found on the living room carpet – no mice were seen.

8   Externally, one of the walls (that of the kitchen) is found to be saturated, as is the external wall to the neighbouring house – 95 Jukes Street – where a broken rainwater gutter is observed.

9   In the bedroom, it was noted that the window overlooked the rear yard to the adjoining property (99 Duncan Street) and that it could be seen that this yard was flooded with sewage emanating from an inspection chamber. There was no access to this yard from the subject property (see Figure 9.1).

Matters to think about

9.02   What steps would you take to investigate the complaint further? Specifically, what evidence would you be seeking and considering to

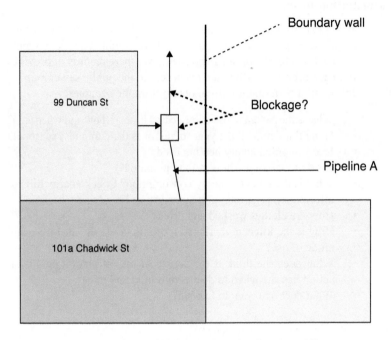

Figure 9.1 The arrows on the solid lines indicate the direction of flow

inform your judgements and decisions in finding answers to the following questions?

What guidance and other documents would you use to reach judgements on:

a   whether the state of the premises amounts to a statutory nuisance (and why);
b   whether any hazards arise under the HHSRS, and if so which;
c   whether the remedial action required is better secured using statutory nuisance or Part 1 of the Housing Act 2004; and
d   the possible remedial action you would require the owner to undertake in order to abate the statutory nuisance and any of the hazards you have identified.

If dealing with the premises under the Environmental Protection Act 1990; which type of abatement notice would you use and why?

If acting under the Housing Act 2004; which course of action(s) would you consider using and why?

Information to seek

9.03   When exactly did the conversion occur? This might indicate which Building Regulations applied, and there might also be possible implications for the drainage problem. Are there records of previous drainage problems? Do you have access to the public sewer map?

9.04   Information you might wish to obtain from the occupier:

- What is the pattern of use of the central heating (how and when etc.)?
- Is the flat damp all the year round, or is the dampness seasonal?
- Is any supplementary heating used?
- Food preparation – how is food prepared?
- What is the level of energy consumption? Check energy bills or information regarding prepayment.
- How are clothes washed and dried?
- How is the kitchen ventilated (other than via the air brick) and mode of use?
- What does she think is the source of the infestation, and what action has she taken to deal with mould and mice?
- What does she want to happen?

9.05   Other information to consider:

- What is the overrun on mechanical ventilation in the bathroom and condition of the extraction equipment (does it draw adequately)?
- What is the relative humidity at the time of visit – is the use of data loggers necessary at this stage?
- Have a damp meter and deep wall probes been used, and what were the readings that would indicate the pattern of dampness? Is the dampness worse on the surface or as the probes go deeper into the wall?
- Has any salts analysis been undertaken from within flat? (Is this necessary at this stage?)
- Should a heat loss assessment be carried out? Is there an EPC and Energy Efficiency Rating? Do you need a heating engineer to report on the size of the boiler (i.e.is boiler adequate)?
- Is the evidence showing condensation as the only form of dampness present?
- Do any other properties in the vicinity have a mouse infestation? What possible points of entry are there to the dwelling?
- What is the fire rating of the entrance door to the flat? Where is this shown? This is not mentioned as a deficiency, so can it be assumed it is adequate? What other fire precautions are in place?

Documentation

9.06 To help you decide on which legislation might be relevant you might consider:

- HHSRS Operating Guidance; BRE Documents such as Digests, Housing and Health International Research Bulletin;
- Malcolm R and Pointing J, 2011, *Statutory Nuisance: Law and Practice*, 2nd edn (Oxford: Oxford University Press);
- LACORS, 2008, Housing – Fire Safety: Guidance on fire safety provisions in certain types of existing housing.

When it comes to understanding defects and specifying works:

- Is there a local standard specification?
- Marshall D, Worthing D, Dann N, and Heath R, 2103, *The Construction of Houses*, 5th edn (Abingdon, Oxon: Routledge).
- Marshall D, Worthing D, Health, R, and Dann N, 2014, *Understanding Housing Defects*, 4th edn (Abingdon, Oxon: Routledge).
- Reddin P (Ed), 2014, *Specifying Minor Works* (Abingdon, Oxon: Routledge).

Courses of action

9.07 The presence of mice and the damp and mould can render the premises "in such a state as to be prejudicial to health". The issue is who is the person responsible? Does statutory nuisance arise from any defect of a "structural character", in which case the owner will be responsible? That might not be the case for the mouse infestation. If there is no evidence that other dwellings are affected and no obvious defects in the property permitting access for the mice, then the occupier would appear to be responsible.

9.08 On the issue of condensation, consider relevant cases.[1] The investigation has to determine that the premises are inherently susceptible to damp and mould to be able to argue that the landlord is responsible. Is the design and construction of the property such that it is capable of dealing with the moisture generated by the occupant? Guidance within the hazard profile in the HHSRS Operating Guidance can provide useful pointers. It should be noted that it is not only the presence of mould (and mould spores) that makes the premises prejudicial to health but also, with elevated relative humidity (rH), there is an increase in the house dust mite population, and the faecal pellets from these organisms are a potent allergen. House dust mites do not breed below an rH of 60%, but when this is exceeded, they start to breed, and this will increase the amount of allergen in the environment. Exposure to high concentrations of these allergens over a prolonged period will cause the sensitisation of atopic individuals.

9.09   So far as the sewerage problem is concerned, the location of the blockage is clearly in a sewer, as the blockage is in a pipeline serving more than one premises. Consequently, the Water and Sewerage Company (WASC) has responsibility for what is and always has been a public sewer because of the age of the property. Even if it were not a sewer, it has left the curtilage of the dwelling, and so it is arguably a public lateral drain.

9.10   If the property had been constructed more recently and pipeline A did not exist – and the adjacent property drained into the pipeline beyond the blockage – then it would still be a public lateral drain, and the WASC would still be responsible. The blockage is at or beyond the inspection chamber; otherwise it would not be discharging sewage. It is possible to act against the WASC by arguing that the state of the premises at 99 Duncan Street is a statutory nuisance, as the result of the blockage in the pipeline for which the WASC is responsible. So, if the WASC is not responsive, a statutory nuisance action would seem to be available for addressing the sewerage problem. You might wish to inform all the affected residents of the action you propose to take to discourage them from spending money unnecessarily.

9.11   Potential HHSRS hazards are: Damp and Mould, Excess Cold, Falling on level surfaces (not covered by statutory nuisance), Domestic Hygiene, Pests, and Refuse, and possibly Fire (the report and information provided does not mention any fire precautions). Also, there is no mention of a Gas Safe Certificate, so is there a potential hazard of Carbon Monoxide etc.? There is no indication of a rating for any of the hazards. Overall, for the problems identified in this property, it would seem that the best option to use is the Housing Act 2004 for addressing all the problems at 101a Chadwick Street.

9.12   Statutory nuisance could not be used to deal with all the problems in 101a Chadwick Street. But if the damp and mould were all the occupier wished to be dealt with, then this could be the best option.

Remedial works in summary

9.13   Works to abate statutory nuisance would be very similar to those set down in any notice served under Part 1 of the Housing Act 2004 for the damp and mould and infestation. These could include: pest proofing (where there are identifiable defects in structure) and/or treatment of infestation; dry-lining of the cold living room walls, plus improved controllable/mechanical ventilation to the kitchen and bathroom, with the kitchen door repaired so that is can be closed properly and with the living room windows overhauled and draughtproofed.

9.14   In a case such as this, were the option to use the Environmental Protection Act 1990 chosen, it would seem unreasonable and poor practice to serve a simple abatement notice under s.80(1) of the Act.

9.15   Whether the local housing authority decides to serve either an Improvement Notice or Hazard Awareness Notice the same remedial action would need to be specified.

9.16   If no fire detection and alarm system is present, then this could be required. A mixed system would need to be installed to ensure a Grade D: LD2 coverage in the common areas and a heat detector in each flat in the room/lobby opening onto the escape route. Additionally, there would need to be (interlinked) Grade D: LD3 coverage in the flat to protect sleeping occupants. A non-interlinked smoke alarm in the lobby opening onto the escape route in the entrance hall of the building would also be required.

9.17   The Housing Act 2004 would also be the only route available for dealing with the trip steps as well as addressing the other hazards identified. If little can be done practically, without unreasonable expense, to deal with the "Falling on Level Surfaces" hazard (the two trip steps), then a Hazard Awareness Notice could be served for that hazard. It rather depends on the hazard rating. If assessed as a Category 1 hazard, then such a notice should be served to meet the statutory duty. If assessed as a Category 2 hazard, then the local housing authority could use its discretion and not take any action. The problem is that a member of the vulnerable age group is in occupation. The provision of grab rails where there are changes of level might reduce the risk.

CASE STUDY 2

9.18   The premises at 64 Fresh Street are a two-storey mid-terrace house constructed in the early twentieth century, with a small front bay at ground floor level. It is entered off the street (front elevation facing East) via a small paved area (approximately 1.5 metres deep, from front gate to front entrance door). The house is made of brick – 9-inch (225-millimetre) solid brick construction. The roof is pitched and tile covered (it has been retiled at some time in the past). The premises comprise: two rooms plus bathroom containing a wash-hand basin and WC on the first floor; and one room plus kitchen/dining on the ground floor (entered directly from the front room). The stairs to the first floor rise from the ground floor front room. The ground floor is of solid construction, and the first floor is of timber construction. Windows are double glazed replacement uPVC to the front elevation (top hung opening light only to all windows) and timber casement replacement windows in the rear wall. The front entrance door and frame are of timber construction. There is a rear paved yard, access to which is via the kitchen. Space heating is by a gas-fired boiler (in the kitchen) and water-filled radiators in the ground floor front room and first floor front room. Hot water is provided by the back boiler. The premises are occupied by a mother and two children, aged eight years (boy) and twelve years (girl).

Inspection findings

9.19   The inspection followed a complaint from neighbours of rubbish in the rear yard. But the EHP carried out a house inspection and found the following matters:

Ground floor front room (living room)

1   Ill-fitting opening light to left window (draughts felt);
2   Loose and ill-fitting uPVC frame to left window;
3   Gas equipment in working order (current gas safety certificate seen but gas safe register not checked);
4   Loose and uneven floor boarding detected under carpeting.

Ground floor rear room (dining/kitchen) (entered directly off the living room)

5   Area of damp affected wall plaster to left (gable) wall;
6   Rotted timber to internal window frame and ill-fitting top casement (not closable);
7   Ill-fitting rear exit door with only a single lock (no bolts);
8   Difficult to reach top opening casement window over the sink unit;
9   Damaged white enamel to kitchen sink, making cleaning difficult.

Staircase and landing to first floor

10   No light switch at foot of stairs for light on first floor landing;
11   Loose handrail to staircase;

12 Access hatch to roof space ill-fitting, allowing draughts (areas of missing and compressed loft insulation, as seen from the opening accessed using folding ladders, and illuminated by flashlight); original insulation appears originally to have been only 50 millimetres thick.

First floor front room (bedroom)

13 Loose and ill-fitting uPVC window frame to left window;
14 Missing catch to opening light to right window.

First floor rear room (bedroom)

15 Single electric socket only;
16 Rotted timber to frame of casement window;
17 Ill-fitting and draughty top hung casement and missing stay to window.

First floor bathroom

18 Evidence of some mould to window frame;
19 Ill-fitting top hung casement window;
20 No source of space heating present;
21 Ill-fitting half-glazed door cannot be easily shut and lacks a bolt with only one flimsy lock.

Rear elevation

22 Rotted timber to ground floor and first floor window frames;
23 Cracked and missing reveal fillets to ground and first floor window frames;
24 Yard gate ill-fitting and insecure;
25 Yard contains an accumulation of household refuse – some loose, some in sacks.

Front elevation

26 Loose and displaced flashing over bay roof and loose roof covering to bay;
27 Front exit door ill-fitting;
28 Loose glazing to light over front door;
29 Rotted timber to bottom of doorframe.

Matters to think about

9.20 The authority should have given notice of entry to the occupier and owner (if a rented property); this will ensure that any action taken that follows the inspection does not fail for lack of notice.

9.21   The initial complaint was about the rubbish, but to comply with statutory duties under both Part III of the EPA 1990 and Part 1 of the
Housing Act 2004, the whole property has been inspected. Whether
this is what would happen in reality will be interesting for readers to
consider. Would the EHP think only of the complaint or use that as
a lead to look at the whole premises? No matter whether thinking of
statutory nuisance or the HHSRS as the basis of the inspection, it is
a whole dwelling assessment.

9.22   No information was provided on ownership or tenure in the scenario, as the legislation does not distinguish between tenures. Notice
of entry would be required even if owner occupied. Tenure only
becomes a consideration when deciding on what is the best course of
action available.

9.23   So the first consideration is to decide whether the state of the premises overall is in such a condition as to be prejudicial to health or a
nuisance. For the nuisance limb of s.79(1) EPA 1990 to apply, there
must be a property boundary crossed; so are neighbours affected? It
might be that only the accumulation in the rear yard – given that it
appears to be comprised of putrescible matter – could be considered,
legally, as a nuisance to neighbours. If the waste is not putrescible,
then visual impact alone cannot render an accumulation or deposit a
nuisance. It could be argued that the accumulation contributes to the
premises being prejudicial to health, as it will attract pests which can
cause disease. In considering whether a pile of refuse and building
waste engages the health limb of statutory nuisance, remember the
words of Lord Widgery CJ:

> *I think that the underlying conception of the section is . . . an
> accumulation of something which produces a threat to health in
> the sense of a threat of disease, vermin or the like.*[2]

9.24   There is a need to investigate further how the waste has accumulated. Is there adequate storage? To determine the cause, the occupier
should be interviewed. Given that the rear yard gate is insecure, is
the accumulation the result of "fly-tipping", or has it arisen from the
occupier not storing refuse properly? Has the occupier ensured that
the refuse is being collected by the local authority? If the occupier is
responsible for the problem, then it does not matter whether they are
a tenant or an owner-occupier.

9.25   It could be that there is no proper provision for waste storage. Note
that s.46 of the EPA 1990 (Receptacles for Household Waste) provides that where a waste collection authority has a "duty by virtue
of section 45(1)(a) above to arrange for the collection of household

waste from any premises, the authority may, by notice served on him, require the occupier to place the waste for collection in receptacles of a kind and number specified". Action could be taken against the occupier (regardless of tenure) to ensure provision of a suitable receptacle for waste storage.

9.26　If there is evidence of pests such as rats or if it is considered that removal of the waste is necessary to prevent any infestation by mice or rats, then action can be taken under the Prevention of Damage by Pests Act 1949, s.4, to secure removal of the waste. Action under the 1949 Act should be taken against the occupier, regardless of tenure.

9.27　Some, but not all, of the items of disrepair noted in the inspection will contribute to the premises being in such as state as to be prejudicial to health. They include those giving rise to cold premises, dampness, and the accumulation of refuse. Service of an abatement notice under s.80(1) EPA 1990 to deal with the refuse problem should be issued against the person responsible: the occupier, which can include a tenant. Abatement notices for statutory nuisances arising from defects of a structural character should be served on the owner.[3]

9.28　Turning to consideration of the premises overall and the possibility of using the Housing Act 2004, are there any hazards in the property? The potential HHSRS hazards arising from the deficiencies (numbered as in the report) are:

a　Excess Cold (Items 1, 2, 6, 7, 12, 13, 15, 16, 17,19 20);
b　Damp and Mould (Items 1, 5, 6, 13, 16, 18, 21, 22, 23, 26, 27, 29);
c　Entry by Intruders (Items 6, 7, 14, 17, 24, 27, 28, 29);
d　Domestic Hygiene Pests and Refuse (Items 25, 27, 29);
e　Food Safety (Item 9);
f　Crowding and Space (bathroom door) (Item 21);
g　Falling on Stairs etc. (Items 10, 11);
h　Falling on Level Surfaces (Item 4);
i　Position and Operability of Amenities (Item 8);
j　Structural Collapse and Falling Elements (Item 28).

9.29　Whether all the potential hazards need to be rated will depend on the extent of the deficiency(ies) and whether the EHP considers that the hazard is worse than the average in the housing stock. Some deficiencies contribute to more than one hazard, whilst some hazards will be reduced by rectifying others. For example, the ill-fitting door to the bathroom will allow water vapour to circulate into the rest of the house and so contribute to the Damp and Mould. The lack of privacy also contributes to the hazard of Crowding and Space.

Repairing and improving the door as part of the work to address the former hazard will also address the latter.

9.30   The hazards have not been rated, although it is highly likely that at least Excess Cold is a Category 1 hazard, and thus the LHA has a duty to take one of the courses of action set down in Part 1 of the Housing Act 2004.

Possible courses of action

9.31   The condition of the rear yard may be addressed by using the statutory nuisance provisions in Part III of the EPA 1990. But these provisions could also be used to address some but not all of the conditions identified. Whether or not the local authority chooses to use the 1990 Act, an occupying tenant is free to use s.82 of the 1990 Act. So if the local authority were to use s.80 for dealing with the accumulation in the rear yard, the tenant could still use s.82 to deal with other forms of statutory nuisance.

9.32   Alternatively, all the matters identified at the property could be addressed by using the Housing Act 2004. This is true even of the accumulation of refuse if there is no adequate provision for waste storage. As the HHSRS Operating Guidance says:

> *there should be suitable and sufficient provision for the storage of refuse awaiting collection or disposal outside the dwelling. There should also be suitable and sufficient provision for the storage of household refuse within the dwelling. The storage provisions should be readily accessible to the occupants, but sited so as not to create a danger to children. The refuse facilities should not cause problems of hygiene, nor attract and allow access to pests.*

The Part 1 provisions in the Housing Act are only available to the local housing authority, and there has been no provision that would permit occupier/tenants to take their own action. This will change from March 2019, when the Homes (Fitness for Human Habitation) Act 2018 (a private members measure introduced by Karen Buck MP) comes into force. This removes any rent limits from s.8 and adds the HHSRS hazards to the criteria for fitness in s.10 of the Landlord and Tenant Act 1985 (implied covenant as to fitness). The standard of fitness here makes no reference to Category 1 or 2 hazards, merely whether the condition is such as to make the dwelling not reasonably suitable for occupation. This will permit tenants to claim for damages or an order for specific performance if any hazards are such as to make the dwelling "unfit".

9.33 As it is by no means certain that all hazards arising would be Category 1 hazards, the local housing authority will have to use its discretion as to which, if any, of the Category 2 hazards it wishes to remedy. For Category 1 hazards, the only decision should be over which of the powers provided under Part 1 should be used.

9.34 It is only at this stage that factors like tenure and type of occupier become a consideration. For example, if the vulnerable age group for Excess Cold were in occupation (people aged sixty-five and over), then an Improvement Notice might be appropriate. Regarding Damp and Mould, should the vulnerable age group (fourteen and under) be in occupation, as is the case here, this will be relevant. For Falling on Stairs etc., the vulnerable age group consists of those of sixty years and over. That said, all ages are vulnerable to the hazards, it is just that certain ages are more so. Therefore, certain hazards such as Excess Cold may have particular significance, given that low-income households will be at risk if they cannot afford to heat the property because it is inherently cold.

9.35 If the property is tenanted, the record of the landlord might be a factor in deciding which course of action to take. The landlord's response when given notice of entry can also be considered. If dealing with a responsible landlord who is agreeable to carrying out the necessary work, an agreement can be confirmed by issuing a Hazard Awareness Notice. Conversely, with a landlord having a poor record of compliance with housing law, an Improvement Notice might be more appropriate (assuming a Prohibition Order is not seen as a better option). It should not be overlooked that the local housing authority may serve different notices for different hazards.

9.36 If the occupier does not want extensive works to be carried out, then the Improvement Notice could be suspended, or, alternatively, a Hazard Awareness Notice could be served on the owner. This possibility is available even for Category 1 hazards. It could be that, after consulting with the occupier, an Improvement Notice (not suspended) is served to address certain hazards, such as Excess Cold, while a suspended Improvement Notice or Hazard Awareness Notice is served with respect to the other hazards.

9.37 Where the occupier also owns the property, the statutory nuisance provisions could be used to address the waste problem in the yard, and a Hazard Awareness Notice could be served to resolve the other deficiencies and hazards.

9.38 This case illustrates that environmental health practitioners have a wide range of options for dealing with residential premises and should not limit themselves to only one route. The principle of using the power thought most likely to resolve the problem is important. As with all types of regulatory enforcement, each case should be judged on its merits.

Notes

1 For example, *GLC v London Borough of Tower Hamlets* [1983] 15 HLR 54; *Dover DC v Farrar* [1980] 2 HLR 32.
2 *Coventry City Council v Cartwright* [1975] 1 WLR 845, 849.
3 Environmental Protection Act 1990, s.80(2)(b).

Index

'reasonable user' 2.33, 4.45; relevant factors' 4.40, 4.45; sound insulation (inadequate) 4.46; standard of proof 4.42; streets and highways 2.31; structural defects 8.06; subjective impressions and observations 4.42; time of day or night 4.40; type of noise 4.40–4.42; *see also* anti-social behaviour; best practicable means; dogs; sound insulation

Northern Ireland 2.07–2.08, 2.30n26, 6.01
notice of intended inspection 5.07–5.10
notice of intention to carry out works 5.06
notices *see* abatement notices; deferred action notices; hazard awareness notices; notice of intended inspection; notice of intention to carry out work; recovery notices; service of notices
'nuisance' limb of statutory nuisance 4.02; high threshold for noise 4.37; history of 2.08; neighbouring property (must be affected) 4.03, 7.02; origins 4.15; premises (state of) 4.19; and public nuisance 4.11; *see also* noise nuisance; private nuisance; public nuisance; statutory nuisance

obsolete (or bad) design 2.10, 4.25
occupation (suitability for) *see* 'reasonably suitable for occupation'
occupiers (of dwellings) 2.10, 8.12; health and safety of 1.07; removal of 7.06; risks to health of 2.10, 7.03; whether or not in lawful occupation 7.06; *see also* tenants
'offensive to the senses': statutory nuisance 4.15
Operating Guidance (H.H.S.R.S.) 7.03
organic compounds Table 5.1
outbuildings 8.10, 8.36
over-crowding: history as a statutory nuisance 2.06; history in housing legislation 3.04n1; structures used for human habitation 2.35; *see also* houses in multiple occupation
'owner' 6.07
owner-occupiers: and grants 3.22–3.23; of unfit houses 3.21

party walls 5.29–5.30
paths *see* footpaths
'person aggrieved' 1.08–1.09, 6.04, 7.01–7.07; drafting of complaints by 7.07; no equivalent in housing legislation 1.09; no need for property rights 4.08; proceedings by 4.27–4.28
personal injuries (risks of): not included in 'health' risks 2.10
personal comfort 4.05; interference with 4.15
'person responsible' (for statutory nuisance) 1.09, 6.07
persuasion and advice: instead of enforcement 1.02; noise nuisance 4.41
pests 1.19, 2.19, 2.24n17, 4.27, 8.29–8.33; Table 5.1
pigeons 2.25–2.26
planning permission (and planning law) 8.10n9; and noise nuisance 4.37
plasterwork (defective) 4.30
plumbing (defective) 4.30
pollution: atmospheric 2.08; industrial 2.05
ponds and pools 2.35, 8.29
"prejudicial to health" 2.08; creature of statute 4.14; definition of 4.17; domestic premises 1.07, 1.09; history of this wording 4.14; narrow interpretation of this wording 7.18; physical injuries (risk of) not included 4.20–4.21; *see also* 'health' limb of statutory nuisance
premises: and abatement notices 6.11; atmospheric emissions from 2.11; defects in 4.27; definition 4.18; domestic 1.06; filthy or unwholesome condition 4.26; fumes and gases emitted from 2.17; internal state of 4.30; layout or design of 4.24; and neighbouring property 4.19; noise emitted from 1.08; "person aggrieved" about state of 7.02; and risks to health 1.07; smoke emitted from 2.15, 2.17; state of 2.04, 2.10, 4.13, 4.18–4.34; visitors to 2.13; workers in 2.13; *see also* industrial, trade, or business premises; property

smells 2.12, 2.22, 4.35, 8.25; and public
nuisance 4.09
smoke 2.11, 2.15–2.17, 4.35
smoke control areas 2.17
soakaways 8.27
soil pipes 8.17
social housing 3.25–3.26; landlords'
liability to prosecution 4.08; tenants'
ability to sue for private nuisance
4.06
soot 2.15
sound insulation 2.10, 4.29, 4.44, 4.46
space heating 3.21–3.22
special grants 3.19–3.20
stability (structural) 3.17
stairs 5.27, 8.06–8.07; Table 5.1
standard grants 3.18–3.19
standard of proof: breaches of
abatement notices 6.28; proceedings
brought by 'person aggrieved' 7.20
statement of reasons 5.47–5.48; and
'better regulation' 5.18
'state of premises' *see* premises
(state of)
statutory nuisance: alternative 'limbs'
of the definition 4.13; compared with
housing law Table 8.1; compared
with private nuisance 4.05; duty of
local authority to inspect for 6.03;
duty of local authority to investigate
complaints 6.03; evidence to justify
service of abatement notice 6.07;
history 2.04–2.12, 2.37; more than
one person can be responsible for
4.31; no fetters on local authority's
discretion to take action 6.03; no
need for victim to have property
rights 4.05; "person responsible for"
6.07; structural defects 6.07; *see also*
'health' limb of statutory nuisance;
'nuisance' limb of statutory nuisance
steam 2.12, 4.36
steps and staircases *see* stairs
storage (for "food preparation") 3.19
strains and cuts (risks of) Table 5.1
streets and highways: cleansing of 2.03;
noise from 2.31
structural defects 4.33; collapse (risk
of) Table 5.1; and noise nuisance
8.05; and smoke 2.17

structures used as dwellings 2.35, 8.09,
8.13
"substantial disrepair" 3.20
"sufferance" 6.07
summary proceedings *see* prosecutions
surveyors: as expert witnesses 4.34
suspensions of notices (or orders) 5.39,
6.20–6.21

tanks *see* water tanks
tax 3.26
tenants: complaints by 3.20; duty as
to use of dwelling-house 5.23; local
authority's advice (and support) to
5.24; personal comfort of 3.20; as
"persons aggrieved" 1.08–1.09, 4.08;
refusal of access by 7.15; right to sue
for Private Nuisance 4.06; vulnerable
1.02, 5.05, 5.63; *see also* occupiers
tents (and similar 'structures') 2.35,
8.12
tenure (changing nature of) 3.25
thermal insulation 7.15
time (of day or night): and noise
nuisance 4.16, 4.40
time-limits (for appeals) 6.18
toilets *see* lavatories; water closets
trade premises 2.05; *see also* industrial,
trade, or business premises
transport facilities 2.29
tree roots 4.05
tribunals *see* first tier tribunals
typhoid 3.01

unfit dwellings: deferred action notices;
and owner-occupiers 3.23; repair or
demolition of 3.18; and tenants in
occupation 3.23; *see also* 'fitness'
standard; slums (and slum clearance)
urban renewal and regeneration 3.20

vans (and similar 'structures') 2.35,
8.12
vehicles 2.31
ventilation 3.11, 3.17, 4.27, 4.30–4.31,
8.03
vermin *see* pests
vessels 4.18
visitors (to premises) 2.13
volatile organic compounds Table 5.1